A Critique
of Pure Marxism

David Simmons

IDEALS and DOGMA

Third Avenue Press

Third Avenue Press
5 Russell Road, Northolt, Middlesex, England.

Designed by Robert Carter.
Illustration on page 6 by Tim Sanders.

Set in 10pt. Times Roman and Gill Sans Bold.

Photocomposition by Tradeset Ltd., Wembley.
Printing and binding by Whitstable Litho, Whitstable.

Contents

Preface

Since the philosophy of Marxism was created, it has been torn by internal contradictions and ambiguities. The first really well-known Marxist tract, *The Communist Manifesto*, preached a coming proletarian revolution which would destroy the capitalist class; naturally enough, it has often been interpreted as a violent revolution. Yet one of the ultimate aims of Marxism is the end of all war, presumably because of the violence and death that war brings. So what is the attitude of Marxism to violence? For or against? Or do Marxists merely assess it according to the context, according to the degree of violence, its necessity, and its justification?

Marx predicted that the development of capitalism, and its increasing harshness to the workers, would force the workers to rise up against it. But Engels noted that the English working class was *"becoming more and more bourgeois"*. And Lenin observed that the workers were not revolutionary by nature; their traditional response to mistreatment has been to unite in trade unions or other associations, to work co-operatively for reform instead of attempting to destroy the whole system. Yet some Marxists still talk of a coming revolution as if it remains an inevitable fact, propelled by historic forces, and consummated by the working class as their only possible response to growing oppression. But history shows that such things do not happen; and Lenin recognised that they couldn't.

But perhaps the most damning contradiction is that although Marxism is a 'left-wing', liberal, even Utopian philosophy, in practice it often degenerates into a form of dictatorship, sometimes of the most powerful and pervasive kind.

These inconsistencies are not mere chance, or due to unforeseen circumstances in real-life development; they are an inherent and inevitable part of Marxism. Because of Marx's philosophical bias, and his excessive respect for the nineteenth century German philosopher, Hegel, he created a system that was rooted in contradictions, based on inconsistencies. Yet paradoxically, this may be one of the greatest strengths of Marxism.

By claiming that the communist revolution is inevitable, it presents itself as a system which is undeniable, impregnable. But at the same time it is possible to claim that popular support can initiate or accelerate the coming revolution, thus offering its adherents a chance to take part in a real and dramatic social change.

Each facet of Marxism has its own psychological appeal, and if some facets are contradicted by others, well, that's life. The net result is a system that can answer all questions, refute all objections, attract all classes. What it loses in logic and rationality, it more than makes up for by its comprehensive appeal; the philosophy with something for everybody.

But in offering something for everyone, ultimately it offers nothing. A genuine science cannot be based on market research, or on self-contradictions. A real philosophy offers truth, not a broad selection of half-truths.

The purpose of this book is to show that the cumulative effect of all the contradictions in Marxism is to totally destroy its value, both as a philosophy, and as a practical method of social change.

I would also like to thank those who helped me write this book, in particular, Robert Richwood, for his useful suggestions, and Eric Blackburn, for his advice on modern Marxism.

1

Connections

The Historical Background

The philosophical roots of Marxism can be traced back over two hundred years to the German philosopher, Gottfried Leibniz, who, although he was not a communist in any way, started a chain of ideas and opinions which ultimately were to lead to the work of Marx.

Leibniz was a skilled mathematician, and created the differential calculus at roughly the same time as Newton came to the discovery. But Leibniz's philosophy was much less factually based. He believed in something he called 'monads'—basic substances that were part of all matter; but unlike the Greek idea of the atom, the monad was a spiritual substance instead of a minute particle.

Aware of the imprecise nature of philosphy, he believed that it should model itself on mathematics, and obtain the same precision and accuracy by arguing from basic axioms, proving its theses and the validity of its discovered truths in a scientific way.

Leibniz's ideas became extremely influential in German universities, partly because of their popularisation by Wolff and Baumgarten; whose work offered a simplistic, exaggerated, and dogmatic view of Leibniz. Immanuel Kant, a private teacher and lecturer, used Leibniz's ideas for many years as a part of his own lectures; but as his opinions developed, he grew increasingly aware of the unsatisfactory nature of Leibniz's work. But Leibniz's reputation was so great that he was, at first, unwilling to launch a direct attack on his ideas.

In 1755 he criticised Wolff's opinion that for everything which existed, there was a valid reason as to why it should be, rather than not be. Kant's reputation also grew, and throughout the following decade he became increasingly critical. In 1764 he published a dissertation, *Natural Theology and Morals*, in which he argued that mathematics has fixed and arbitrary definitions, clearly defined operations, and concepts that are based in reality. Philosophy, he said, could never attain such precision, and should stick to analysing reality with intellectual tools.

Leibniz also believed that the human mind, using only the power of logic and thought, could obtain knowledge about things which could not be perceived by the senses directly, such as abstract ideas or deities. If these things cannot be seen or perceived in any way, then we can have no empirical knowledge of them; but Leibniz believed that factual data was unnecessary—all that was needed was thought.

The year before his thesis on natural theology, Kant had attacked the idea that one could prove the existence of God from logic alone. Seven years after that, in 1770, he criticised the view that the senses are a primitive form of thought, and a source of knowledge in themselves. But it was not just Leibniz's ideas that Kant rejected, but his whole way of thinking; his logic, his categories, and his methods for defining different aspects of reality. What Kant disputed was the entirety of Leibniz's system, from the basic principles to the final conclusions; and a disagreement of such an extent needed an absolutely comprehensive refutation.

Kant's answer was the *Critique of Pure Reason*, a massively unreadable volume which analysed the roots of scientific knowledge in the realms of mathematics, physics, and metaphysics. Maths and physics both dealt with reality—in different ways, and with different tools, but they both investigated a reality that human beings could actually perceive. Metaphysics on the other hand was cut off from reality, from sensory experience; therefore it was unable to make what Kant called *a priori*, synthetic judgements. That is, it was unable to make judgements which were logically independent of the senses, and it was unable to make statements which were not already implicit in the existing argument.

Nor was it possible to derive information independently of known facts. For every statement that could be made on behalf of a thesis not rooted in empirical data, another opposite statement could be made. Both thesis and antithesis could have equally good reasons put forward in support of their validity, and both could be proved with the same amount of evidence; that is, no empirical evidence whatsoever. And if two conflicting arguments are given, then one, or both of them, must be false.

Kant delayed publication of his *Critique* for ten years as he tried to refine the logic and clarity of his arguments, but he was working within a tradition and method that was not conducive to clarity. His work was widely misunderstood, and he went on to re-write the *Critique*, and write a monograph explaining the ideas contained in it. Not surprisingly, there were also many who deliberately mis-interpreted Kant's work, who wished to maintain that Leibniz was still the most important German philosopher. There was even one writer who argued that Kant's reasoning had actually been anticipated by Leibniz.

There were also developments from Kant's ideas; Georg Wilhelm Hegel argued that Kant was mistaken in regarding the contradictions between thesis and antithesis as disproof of one or both of them. Hegel claimed that contradictions were an essential feature of human reasoning; they were the means by which knowledge progressed. The actual process was described as a dialectical one, that is, based on argument; first a thesis is put forward, then its opponents point out its contradictions and offer an antithesis, an opposite theory; finally a new theory is proposed—a synthesis—containing elements of both.

Whereas Kant argued that contradictions invalidated one argument or another, and should be avoided in rational analysis, Hegel claimed that they were acceptable, even beneficial. Contradictions were the force which propelled scientific development, and so should not be avoided, nor should there be any attempts to eliminate them from a theory.

Hegel's other ideas—on the role of the state, the nature of reality, the forces behind historical development, or the possibility of a scientific study of society or philosophy, all made a profound impact on a Germany that was still recovering from the Thirty Years War. Also, as well as being influenced by Leibniz, Hegel was following in the same spiritual, anti-empirical tradition as him. Hegel's most enduring creation was a direct result of Kant's work, but his contemporary popularity was due more to his continuity with Leibniz.

The new ideas which Hegel had developed were soon acclaimed and applied in almost every academic realm, with schools of thought ranging from Hegelian ethics to Hegelian jurisprudence. His ideas were particularly influential at the University of Berlin, where he spent his last years, up to 1831.

In 1835 a seventeen year old named Karl Marx, the son of a Prussian lawyer, left home to study law at the University of Bonn. He acquired problems rather than academic success, and the following year he transferred to the University of Berlin. Marx attended lectures by Savigny on jurisprudence, and Eduard Gans' lectures on criminal law. Savigny was not a Hegelian, but sympathised with a number of his views; Gans on the other hand was a committed Hegelian, and through his lectures Marx came to see jurisprudence and philosophy in a new light. In order to understand and assess Hegel's value, Marx devoted himself to a full-time study of Hegel's work. After three weeks of continuous reading he was converted; he gave up law, and took up philosophy.

Marx was more successful as a student at Berlin, and his reputation was spreading through the literary and academic circles in which he moved, partly because of his polemical, and occasionally atheistic, articles. His fame was growing, and in 1841 he was invited to contribute to the *Rheinische Zeitung*, within a few months he was made editor of the paper. His hostility towards the oppressive Prussian regime brought increasingly strict censorship to bear on the paper, and in April 1843 the *Zeitung* was banned. That same month he married Jenny von Westphalen, and together they decided to leave Germany for France; Marx had no family ties, his journalistic career was ended, and he had little chance of an academic career in Prussia. Then he was offered the post of editor on the *Deutsch-Französische Jahrbücher*; he accepted immediately, and in the November of that year left for Paris.

Paris in the 1840s was not only a more liberal, enlightened place than Prussia—it was also the centre of another radical tradition; not a philosophical one, but a practical, revolutionary tradition. One of its leading lights had been Francois Noel Babeuf, who, in addition to preaching revolution, believed that all men had equal rights to property, and to all the fruits of nature. He also believed that following the revolution, government should be in the hands of *"a small body of convinced and ruthless individuals, who were to wield dictatorial power and educate the proletariat until it reached a level at which it comprehended its proper task."*[1] Babeuf formed a secret society to overthrow the Directorate, but its plans were discovered, and Babeuf was arrested and executed. Babeuf's colleague, Filipo Buonarotti, communicated some of these ideas to Louis-Auguste Blanqui, an ardent revolutionary, and the creator of a number of secret societies. Blanqui had no

1. Isiah Berlin *Karl Marx,* Oxford University Press.

theoretical explanations for his ideas, but this did not affect the strength of his convictions, his determined but vague belief in revolution, equality, and the abolition of religion.

One of Blanqui's adherents was Wilhelm Weitling, who believed in an overtly violent class war, with the poor fighting the rich—with the battle led by the very lowest strata of society, misfits, criminals, and the grindingly poor—those with nothing to lose. In 1843, Weitling, along with a small group of German exiles, formed 'The League of The Just.' To distinguish themselves from the reformist socialist groups, they described themselves as being 'communists.'

It was at this time that Marx received some economics articles for his paper, sent in by a wealthy German radical named Friedrich Engels. Engels was the son of a rich cotton manufacturer, and so was an insider to many of the processes and policies which Marx was eager to study—the actual workings of capitalism. Engels had first-hand experience both from his father's cotton mill, and from a study he had done of labour conditions in Britain; his knowledge of practical capitalism was detailed and comprehensive. Marx had studied the theories of economics and philosophy—but knew little of the actual day to day operations. Together they could create a total understanding of the system.

In 1845 Marx was expelled from Paris, and went to Brussels, where he met some members of the now-dissolved 'League of the Just': the remaining members had gone to England and formed a 'German Worker's Educational Society.' When Marx went to England he was introduced to the group by Engels, and was much impressed; not only did they share many ideas about the need for change, but they also had as their goal the actual implementation of change. Marx returned to Brussels to form a similar group, while Engels formed another group in Paris.

In 1847 the three groups met in London, and was decided that they form an international 'Communist League', and commission a detailed party platform, to be presented at a second meeting later in the year. By this time Marx and Engels were quite influential members of the League, and so they were asked to write the party's platform; it was published the following year, with the title, *The Manifesto of the Communist Party*. It proposed—in vaguely, but theatrically phrased terms—the abolition of private property, and the centralisation in the hands of the state, all means of production, all banking, sources of credit, transport, communication, and agriculture.

Marx continued his research, seeking the laws by which society operated, and seeking to demonstrate that communism was the only valid and equitable form of society that could exist. His attacks on capitalism grew more precise as he accumulated specific examples of its faults, and his theories on the laws of society grew more and more comprehensive as he assimilated the ideas of Hegel, Ricardo, Adam Smith, Babeuf and others into his personal scheme of things. He developed the theory of surplus value, as an explanation of the means by which workers are exploited; he deduced laws on the accumulation of capital, to show that exploitation must continue, and grow more severe; and he formulated a law of historic development, that capitalist society must progress towards a dictatorship of the proletariat.

According to his own correspondence there is little that he claims to have created himself. *"What I did that was new was to prove: 1) that the existence of classes is only bound up with particular historical phases in the development of production; 2) that the class struggle necessarily leads to the dictatorship of the proletariat; 3) that this dictatorship itself only constitutes the transition to the abolition of all classes and to a classless society."*[1]

Marx and Engels also distinguished between socialism and communism in a different way from their predecessors;

---

1. Karl Marx, in correspondence to J. Weydemeyer, 1852.

socialism was a bourgeois revolution, but communism was a working class revolution, led and support by the proletariat. They also predicted—or at least suggested—that the revolution would be a violent one, a *"forcible overthrow of all existing social conditions."*[1]   The Russian revolution fitted both of these descriptions; it was fought against an oppressive, exploitative regime, and violence seemed to be the only possible method of social change. Gradually Russia came to be the showpiece of communism—if only because it was the only working example of it. But this in itself was enough; one of the tenets of the old nineteenth century liberal capitalism was that no other system, apart from capitalism, was even workable. The success of the Russian revolution destroyed the last remnants of liberal capitalism, and offered a completely new view of how society could be run.

By the 1930s Western intellectuals were regular visitors to Russia, and many respected thinkers returned much impressed with the success of the new regime. But all that had been achieved was 'socialism in one country'; the 1936 Soviet Constitution recognised implicitly that the country was at the stage of the dictatorship of the proletariat— socialism in the sense of its being the transitional phase leading towards communism. The only trouble being that it was a transitional phase which could not be passed; the dictatorship of the proletariat had become a police state controlled by Stalin. As early as 1921 the state had taken to shooting its dissidents, and by 1936 Stalin's purges had reached a scale that would have horrified the Western intellectuals had they known.

But the revolution was an apparent success; if nothing else, the control of the state had passed from one set of hands to another, and the predictions of Marx and Engels had been borne out. This success was no doubt a contributing factor

1. Marx and F. Engels.   *The Manifesto of the Communist Party.*

in subsequent revolutions—although in those countries which developed independently of Russia, such as China, Yugoslavia, and Cuba, different structures were tried for the economy and the society. Under Mao the Chinese economy was very much a decentralised one, while current developments are taking it in the direction of state-owned capitalism. After Tito's break with Stalin the Yugoslavian state has had an ever decreasing share of the economy, as ownership has passed into local hands.

But are the new communist states successful because of Marxism, or because they have rejected it? Was the failure of the Russian example merely a colossal piece of back luck —that a potentially democratic country should come to be dominated in its early years by a megalomaniac? Or is the chaos that surrounds the forcible transfer of power a natural environment for those who seek power? Or to generalise, are Marx's rules on historical development no more than tendencies or possibilities, or are they genuinely scientific laws?

If Marxism is totally scientific, then its laws and goals must be treated with respect as an ideology which analyses, explains, and gives practical policies for change. If it is not— or only partially—scientific, then those parts of it with no empirical or rational basis must be discarded; an erroneous plan of action can do more damage to society than no action at all.

The scientific validity of Marxism will be the subject of the next chapter.

2

The Owl of Minerva

Marxism as a Science

There is little that any author can write on the scientific validity of Marxism that has not already been covered by Sir Karl Popper, but any useful additions that can be made will be included here. What will be useful is an analysis of Maurice Cornforth's refutation of Popper's work; this offers the opportunity to re-assess Popper's work, while at the same time examining the scientific validity of Marxism.

One of Cornforth's main criticisms is that Popper attacks not what Marxism *is*, but what Popper *says* Marxism is. This is a serious allegation, and if true would seriously restrict the validity of Popper's critique. Any meaningful criticism of a theory must point out the errors of fact and logic contained in the theory. If a theory can be shown to have a series of failures of fact and logic, then its conclusions become uncertain, to say the least; the greater the number of errors, the less the theory can be relied on. If the critique is based on a misunderstanding or misinterpretation of the theory, then one is not criticising the theory, but an inaccurate version of it. And if the criticisms do not relate to errors in the theory itself, they equally can have no significant bearing on the ultimate conclusions that the theory arrives at. Thus, the criticism is irrelevant or meaningless.

An allegation as serious as this should have been sub-stantiated with specific examples of misquoting or misinterpretation, 1) to prove that it occurred, and 2) to demonstrate the degree of misrepresentation, and hence, the degree of inaccuracy of the criticism. Cornforth alleges that Popper has given an incorrect view of Marxism, but fails to give any detailed proof—except by occasionally quoting Hegel or Marx as saying something different from what Popper claims they said. But as the writings of both Hegel and Marx contained many contradictions and ambiguities, and their ideas changed over the years, such quotations do not always carry much weight.

In addition, Popper was careful to distinguish in his criticism between the actual opinions of Marx, and those whom Popper describes as *"Vulgar Marxists,"* or *"Radical Marxists."* Thus, in criticising Marxism Popper is not always criticising Marx. The only complaint that could reasonably be made is that Popper did not specify exactly who he meant by *"Vulgar Marxists."* But this does not affect the validity of Popper's critique of Marx.

Popper's major criticism is that Marxism is not scientific; and as Marxists like to regard their ideology as a science, an attack of this sort is fundamental. The basis of Popper's charge is his principle of falsifiability; that is, that any scientific theory should be open to falsification. The traditional method of establishing a theory has been by verification; observing true examples of the theory's working. Thus, if one says that heavy objects fall down when they are dropped, or that all swans are white, then if observation showed that swans *were* white and that heavy objects *did* fall when dropped, then the theory was considered to be proved. A theory was established by the repeated observation of what is predicted.

This may seem perfectly reasonable, but as a method of establishing the ultimate truth of a scientific theory it is not actually very satisfactory. Because no matter how many observations occur agreeing with the theory, there is always the possibility of a contrary observation. For example, anyone who drops a heavy object while in a plane in free fall, or in an orbiting space capsule will find that it may not fall down; because gravity no longer affects things in the same way. Equally, the discovery of Australia showed that swans are not always white—as people had once believed—they can be black. So the final truth of a theory is not demonstrated by repeated verification, no matter how many times it is verified, because the next example may merely disprove the theory.

Popper suggested that a more meaningful way of establishing the validity of a theory is by discovering whether or not it can be falsified. That is, it must be *open* to disproof. It does not actually have to be disproved, but it should phrase its statements and predictions with such precision that certain events *would* disprove it. And it should definitely not be phrased in such a way that regardless of what happens, the theory can accommodate it. If a theory can accept any event without its supporters admitting it has been disproven, because they can reinterpret it, then equally one can say that no event proves the theory. It can accommodate all events, so its descriptions are not unique to any particular set of events. Its validity is not related in any way to the real world, therefore it is meaningless. If it can be neither proven nor disproven it is not a scientific theory.

Cornforth objected to this blunt exclusion of Marxism from the realms of science, claiming that Popper wanted to play God, deciding for himself which theories are scientific. Cornforth's more practical objections were 1) scientists do not work in the way Popper describes, 2) if we do not accept the truth of anything until it is absolutely proven we can allow few practical uses of science, and 3) many accepted theories are not open to falsifiability.

As regards how scientists work, this is not actually Popper's primary concern. The principle of falsifiability is not related to the specific methods of investigation used by scientists, nor in the general principles followed, nor in the actual thought processes of those engaged in research. Popper's work was aimed at creating a philosophy of science, an epistemology, not a methodology or a psychology; its aim is to find a basis for establishing the ultimate truth of science, not to show how any given scientist arrives at his particular view of the truth.

And the practical applications of science—building bridges is the example Cornforth uses—are not science at all, but technology, the applied use of science. Modern knowledge of engineering, metallurgy, inorganic chemistry, etc, is sufficiently well established for us to regard it as 'truth' in the ordinary sense of the word—the principles are acceptable, put into practice they work, and there is no reason whatsoever to disbelieve their correctness. But that is another thing from establishing their *absolute* truth. Perhaps many of the principles used in current technology will never be disproved, but scientists consider it necessary to have some way of ascertaining the ultimate validity of a theory, and for that we need a philosophy of science, a way of investigating the rules which science must follow.

Finally, Cornforth states that *"the general theory of relativity, the laws of thermodynamics and the theory of evolution by natural selection are scientific theories which, though well confirmed, and fundamental in modern science, are not readily responsive to Dr. Popper's simple criterion of 'falsifiability'."*[1]

Although I cannot claim to be a scientist, and cannot fully answer Cornforth's statement, it is clear from just background reading on these subjects that he is at least partly in error. The second and third laws of

---

1. M. Cornforth   *The Open Philosophy and the Open Society,* Lawrence and Wishart.

thermodynamics may not be falsifiable, but the first law states that energy can be neither created or destroyed; this is a specific statement, and as such, can be proven false; but no actual example of disproof has ever occurred.

And if Cornforth were referring to Darwin's theory of evolution he would be correct; but Darwin's work has long been superseded by modern biology, and its studies of inherited characteristics, adaptation to the environment, and evolution by adaptation.

But Cornforth is most clearly in error when he refers to the theory of relativity; that is one of the most precise formulations of knowledge in the realm of physics. And from its precision come predictions—and, of course, any theory that makes predictions lays itself open to being falsified, should the predictions be proved incorrect.

One of the principles of the general theory of relativity is that the path of a ray of light curves in the presence of a gravitational field. This has the effect of moving the apparent position of a star whose light has passed through a gravitational field on its way to us. Thus, a ray of light from a distant star passing by our sun would be pulled in towards the sun by its field of gravity; and the apparent image would move outwards—by a very specific amount— *"1·7 seconds of arc."*[1] The way to test this would be by noting the position of a particular star when its light had passed through no known field, and then noting its new position when its light had passed through a known gravitational field—our sun. And the best time to do this would be during a solar eclipse, so that the glare of the sun did not blank out or distort any images.

Three years after the general theory of relativity was published, two groups of astonomers set off to observe the total eclipse of the sun—the one that would occur on May 29, 1919. They photographed a number of stars, and

1. Albert Einstein *Relativity*, Methuen.

comparisons of the photos taken during the eclipse and photos taken under normal conditions showed that the stars did appear to move—as predicted by Einstein—and the amount of movement was also in accordance with the theory. This was only the first verification of that one particular aspect of the general theory; since 1919 dozens of other observations have confirmed the displacement of light, the latest being by the National Observatory, Greenbank, West Virginia, in 1979. Other observations have provided proof of two entirely different aspects of the general theory.

Einstein made very specific predictions, each one of which laid his theory open to falsification. The first law of thermodynamics contains two predictions, and modern experiments on inherited characteristics are in effect a series of predictions. All that can be said is that perhaps Cornforth is correct regarding the second and third laws of thermodynamics. But whether or not these two laws are *"fundamental in modern science"* is something that neither Cornforth nor the present writer are qualified to answer.

Having denied that the principle of falsifiability is valid, Cornforth goes on to deny that Marxism has ever been proved false. Marx postulated that society developed from Feudalism, via capitalism, to communism; the prediction was then, that communism would first appear in the advanced capitalist countries. But the first revolution occurred in Russia, a backward feudal country; does this not disprove the theory? Well, no; certain things hadn't been taken into account, and of course, 'a chain breaks at its weakest link'.

Cornforth explains that this does not constitute a reversal of any sort; at no time did Marx or any Marxists formulate any laws of historic inevitability. It's just that *"the materialist conception of history formulates explanatory generalisations about how human society always develops*.[1] No predictions are made; he argues that the general principles of materialist dialectics do not make any forecasts. The principles involved merely describe certain general tendencies, and if the situation within a country changes radically, then its probable future development also changes. The general tendencies remain valid, even if the time for their development, or the sequence in which they occur, are indeterminate.

This latter explanation would be perfectly reasonable—circumstances do change—but Marx did claim to have discovered laws relating to society's operations, and laws do not change with circumstances. Laws are fixed and immutable, and are a completely different category from tendencies. Nor, in referring to the fundamentals of his theory, did Marx speak of tendencies, or probabilities; he spoke of laws. He states, *"this law follows: the mass of the surplus value produced is equal to . . .", "This is the absolute general law of capitalist accumulation"*, and *"The law by which a constantly increasing quantity of means of production . . .", "The production of surplus value is an absolutely necessary law . . .",* and *"The law of capitalist accumulation . . . is such as to forbid any decline in the degree of exploitation of labour . . ."*[2]

No ifs, buts, or maybes; no perhaps, probably, or usually. When Marx described the basic tenets of his system he spoke of laws. He also made predictions; as mentioned in the last chapter, he stated that *"the class struggle necessarily leads to the dictatorship of the proletariat"*. This statement was not mere rhetoric as far as Marx was concerned; it was a fact, based on the fundamental laws of capitalism.

1. M. Cornforth, op. cit.
2. Karl Marx *Capital*.

According to Marx, the source of capitalist exploitation was surplus value, the value of production created by a worker, in excess of the value he was paid. The worker is paid only enough for basic subsistence, while the capitalist acquires the surplus values produced by a number of workers.

The worker's earnings are limited by his lack of bargaining power, but the capitalist's income is limited only by the number of workers he can employ. But he also needs to accumulate ever-increasing quantities of capital in order to compete effectively with other capitalists; this requires an ever-growing degree of exploitation of the workers. There is a corresponding deterioration in the workers' living standards, and their only response is ultimately to rise up, and seek a *"forcible overthrow of all existing social conditions"*.[1] This prediction was based on laws, not mere opinions; laws which were related to one another in a logical sequence, and leading inexorably to one specific conclusion. To the conclusion that communism must grow out of advanced capitalism. And where specifically, would it appear? *"In England, the revolutionary process is plain to all who have eyes to see."*[2] At that time England was the most advanced capitalist nation in the world, and if Marx's laws were valid, then England was the place where the laws would prove themselves in practice. But the laws were not proved valid, and the revolution occurred instead in Russia.

But according to modern Marxists, the laws have not been disproved. 'The chain breaks at its weakest link.' In answer to the failure of supposedly inexorable scientific laws, we have a cliché. Certainly, Marx was justified in interpreting the events of his time in the way that he did; capitalism exploited, oppressed, and mistreated the workers to a degree that was inhumane. But he was not justified in assuming that the degree of exploitation would worsen, nor was he correct

1. Marx and Engels *The Manifesto of the Communist Party.*
2. Karl Marx *Capital.*

in claiming that scientific laws were involved. As Bamford Parkes puts it, Marx made the mistake of thinking that the problems of capitalism in its infancy were also those of its old age.

Nonetheless, Marxism has failed the test of falsifiability; but can it claim to be scientific in the traditional sense? Here also the answer is no. Non-corroborative examples of some predictions have occurred, while no instances have occurred which corroborate Marx's predictions. There have been no examples of advanced capitalist countries undergoing a communist revolution nor have their been any examples of socialist countries evolving into full-fledged communism. But this does not necessarily invalidate the whole theory, as it is still possible for some aspects of it to be confirmed. But the likelihood of any confirmation occurring in the manner predicted is very slim.

It is possible that the degree of accumulation of capital has increased since the time of Marx, but there would be immense difficulties in measuring the degree of concentration existing at that time. And it would be almost as troublesome attempting to assess the proportion of wealth owned by the rich at the present time. It is more likely that the concentration of capital has actually decreased; and certainly there has not been the steady impoverishment of the workers that Marx prophesied. The best that could be said of the scientific value of Marxism is that where it has not actually been disproved, it is doubtful.

So on what basis is it scientific? According to Cornforth, the strength of Marxism comes from its materialism and its dialectical approach. But the meaning of materialism as it is used here is not the same as that which is regarded as the ideology of capitalism. The word is used here to describe a philosophy, an approach to study, a way of examining the world around us. The materialist method is to study events and objects with the view that the structure of the material world is the main influence on the ideas, aims, and purposes that develop within that world. The physical environment creates and forms the mental environment.

At some points that argument for materialism degenerates into claims that philosophical study must be on materialist lines because of the logal flaws in idealism. Again, the word 'idealism' is not being used in its ordinary sense; in this case it means a belief that an understanding of the material world must come from a study of the aims and ideals that have formed it. Thus, in materialism, the physical world is regarded as being the first and primary cause of events; in idealism it is the mental, non-material phenomena that are the agents of change.

The excessive claims that are made for materialism seem to revolve primarily around the flaws in religion, the excess being in the fact that materialism is claimed to be more scientific than religion—something which is not a science in any way. It is one thing to attack religion for its belief in a 'soul' or a 'heaven', to claim that these things do not exist, and that with a scientific attitude one has a more rational, intelligent approach to the world. But it is quite another thing to say that because religion has logical flaws in it, materialism is the best mode of science. The validity of religion is not relevant because it is not a science, and therefore cannot be used as the basis of any comparison of different types of scientific method.

But independently of what it is compared to, there are still many other objections to materialism. In its pure form materialism excludes psychological motives from any analysis of events; everything is to be explained in physical terms—the forces of production, the means of production, the accumulation of capital, and the need to acquire things (food etc) in order to live. Pure materialism does not accept that non-material abstractions like motive, belief, or nostalgia, greed, altruism, megalomania, gregariousness, or egoism have any place in a rational scheme of understanding. What drives people to act as they do is nothing but a simple response to the multiple forces of the environment.

Cornforth makes it quite clear that in his opinion, any philosophy which is a mixture of idealism and materialism must be an unsatisfactory mixture. He also states that Marxism *"adopts a consistently materialist approach to all questions . . ."*[1] Although both Shlomo Avineri (a Marxist) and Karl Popper (not a Marxist) have stated that Marx himself was not a total materialist, that his philosophical position was somewhere in between the two extremes. Popper states that although Marx's teachings are associated with such phrases as 'class interest' and 'economic motives', the idea that these are actually the 'driving forces of history' is a gross misinterpretation of Marx; and it is at this stage that Popper introduces the phrase, *"Vulgar Marxist"*.

But of course, there is no reason to believe that the attitudes of modern Marxists must be identical with the teachings of Marx. So, the modern tendency is to be exclusively materialist. No compromise is possible; either one explains the entire world, all the events that occur, and all the decisions that are taken, in idealist terms, or one explains them in materialist terms.

In Marxist eyes it is no use seeking a material explanation of the forces that power a train, and then accepting a psychological explanation of why all little boys want to become train drivers. It would not be considered rational to accept a physical explanation of the laws of fluid dynamics, the workings of a diesel engine, and the operation of an ocean liner, and then allow a non-physical reason why some people leave comfortable surroundings to help the poor of the Third World. There cannot be two separate methods,

1. M. Cornforth, op. cit.

one for one aspect of the world, and one for another aspect; the world is one thing, therefore there can be only one basic way of understanding it.

The exclusion of psychology means that materialist Marxists can never fully appreciate the value of the subject. They either simplify it to the level of physical experiments, usually involving rats running through mazes, or they ignore it completely. And in doing so they exclude from their own studies everything that could explain why people act in particular ways, why they seek social change, personal power, promotion, friendship, status, or wealth. So they are not capable of suitably rephrasing Marxist theory to allow for the many forms of human nature.

Most importantly, they exclude the possibility of their proposed system having compensatory mechanisms to protect the people from the psychological defects of the powerful. If personal motives do not exist, then they cannot be harmful. If the rulers have no potentially dangerous attitudes, then there is no reason to worry about giving them absolute power. But not everyone who enters politics is capable of running a country effectively and efficiently. There are even politicians who are not very nice people; they have purges, show trials, they persecute their opponents or minority groups, and ignore the needs of the majority of the people.

The problem is not one of total lunatics gaining power, but of fairly normal people, with stronger drives and opinions than most, actively seeking power. And anyone who actively seeks great power is almost certainly not qualified to wield it. But even quite normal people, if placed in such a position, would find themselves insulated from the citizens who were subject to their decisions, and insulated from the effects of their decisions. To find out what things were really like could take quite an effort of information gathering, and touring the countryside. When considering the possession of absolute power, even mild laziness could be a social disaster; full-blown paranoia could be a first grade catastrophe.

To compensate for the various perversities of human nature, western democracies have, over the years, equipped themselves with a number of balancing mechanisms, to ensure that power is distributed fairly evenly. The state is usually split up into both central and local government, and the people elect members for both these; so if any particular group or person misbehaves, they can be thrown out. There is an independent judiciary, to ensure that people are subject to justice, and not to the arbitrary whim of a ruler. And the transmission of news and information is also independent of the state, to ensure that people are not restricted to a totally biased view of events. These mechanisms may not be perfect, but they are infinitely better than the total absence of restraints.

Nor can a materialist theory offer a society rationally constructed for the benefit of human beings, since by its very definition it excludes the one subject that studies human beings as individuals. A system that does not understand people cannot work effectively for people. If it does not understand their differences, their idiosyncrasies, and their preferences, it cannot be expected to cope with these things, to provide a full range of goods and services for the intellectual, aesthetic, and emotional needs of the people. It has been said that Marxism is fine in theory, but it doesn't take human nature into account; in doing this it is omitting the most important aspect of any social theory—people. The whole purpose of any social theory is to create an environment for people to live happily in; a theory which deliberately ignores how people think cannot assess what will make them happy—and therefore will be less able to provide what is needed.

The emphasis on materialism is one of the major faults of Marxism, but it is only a serious fault because of the extreme claims that are made. Normally we seek understanding of the world through the relevant field of science; the stresses on the wing of an aeroplane can be explained via aerodynamics, the types of metal needed to withstand the stress can be found through metallurgy, and the best way of constructing a wing can be discovered using the techniques of engineering. No single approach can cover everything; unless we speak in the most generalised terms. Then there is one way—by obtaining facts, seeking logical, perhaps causal, relationships between them, analysing events in a logical manner, and trying to ascertain the truth in all cases —in other words, the scientific method.

There are two possible deductions from the Marxist claim of materialism; either they are saying that their theory is a science because they use the scientific method, and they just happen to have another word for it, or else they are claiming that only they have the true scientific method. In the first case, their term would be redundant, and no more than a source of confusion. There is no inherent value in using an excess of words, although if they wanted to they could describe their philosophy as being Marxist materialist orthodox pragmatic empirical non-carcinogenic rationalism. The name would then include a more compre-hensive description of the ideas involved. But a name is rarely, if ever, a description; nor does it need to be. The second possibility—that only Marxists have the true method —would be arrogant, were it correct; but there are no indications that Marxists have taken their claims that far.

Cornforth states that no theory can be accepted as valid unless it is materialist; certainly, all modern physical science operates via the study of physical objects, so in that sense, science is materialist. But this does not mean that materialism is scientific. To claim that one studies the world and its phenomena through their material relations is a claim of no great significance. Any conventional scientist would make the same claim, but he would relate it to his own field, using the terminology of his subject. For example, an astronomer might say, "I am studying a star to see if there are any variations in its movement that might be explained by gravitational influences." In other words, what he studies are material things and the physical effects they have on one another. But to emphasise the material aspect of the study would be redundant, simply because it is so obvious.

On the other hand, it is possible to study the material world and *not* be scientific. Just because science is materialist, it does not mean that all materialism is science. All cats are animals, but not all animals are cats. The Flat Earth Society studies the material world, but few would call them scientific. That description comes from the way investigations are carried out, not from the name given to them.

So why did Marx emphasise the materialist aspect of his work? The reason is that he wanted to distinguish his philosophy from that of Hegel, who was an idealist. In the introduction to *Capital*, Marx states that his own *"dialectical method is not only different from the Hegelian, but is its direct opposite."* Hegel believed in a hidden reality, beyond that of the real and observable world. He believed in unseen 'Essences' or 'Ideals' inside each physical object, and these 'Ideals' were constantly changing for the better, moving towards the 'Absolute Ideal'. At the same time the 'Ideals' were pulling the physical bodies in which they resided, with them, towards the absolute. And this applied not just to everyday objects—the whole of society was subject to the force of these 'Essences'. In ordinary terms, his view was that change came from within, and where man sought to create change it was because of the influence of the 'Ideal'. Unknown to him, man's soul or spirit was pushing him towards actions that were in accordance with the ultimate goal of change.

Marx had learnt Hegelian philosophy as a student, and perhaps because of his youth, or perhaps because it was the first all-encompassing philosophical scheme he had come across, he readily absorbed the Hegelian doctrines. He remained a Hegelian for some years, until the work of Feuerbach caused him to re-assess Hegel's work. But many of Marx's basic ideas are strongly Hegelian in tone; Popper lists nine items from Hegel's philosophy which Marx had incorporated into his own, ranging from historicism to the dialectical method. And McClellan cites as evidence of the continuity of Marx's work, the fact that the *Grundrisse* is as Hegelian as the Paris Manuscript.

And it is the Hegelian basis of Marxism that is the cause of most of its faults, especially its many internal contradictions. As mentioned in the last chapter, contradictions were not something that Hegel disapproved of, or even avoided; after all, absolute truth would emerge from the contradictions of the dialectical method. Similarly, Marx believed that communism, the absolute social system, would develop out of the dialectical processes of society. Hegel believed in the historic development of the real world; Marx believed in the historic inevitability of communism.

But in taking Hegelian patterns of thought, Marx was also taking up a totally irrational system of philosophy. Unlike Toynbee, Hegel wrote about the historic development of things without having any real understanding of history. Unlike Machiavelli, Hegel wrote about the state without having any personal experience of the state's operations. Hegel possessed limited knowledge, and even less logic; so Marx inherited, or took over, a system which lacked any firm logical foundation, any rigourous analysis of one's beliefs, any realisation of the need to state one's premises, logic, and conclusions in a clear, concise, and precise way. One of the characteristics that Hegel shares in common with many latter-day Marxists, is their irrational convoluted way of expressing things; although this is less true of Marx—with the turgid exception of the *Grundrisse*—which is simply the rough draft of an unfinished manuscript, and was not intended to be published in its existing form.

Marxist arguments are rarely laid out on a linear fashion, taking a fact and then making deductions from it, or taking two facts and seeing if a third can be deduced. The Marxist method is a combination of polemic and rhetoric, often expressed in the most verbose and unintelligible terms possible. For example—   *"But if Marx does not accept the Hegelian identification of bureaucracy with universality, he still retains the dialectical concept of a* 'universal class', *i.e. a partial social stratum which is, however, an ideal subject of the universal concept of the* Gemeinwesen.*"*[1]

It is possible that the faults of Marxism stem from an inability to express things clearly; it is equally likely that the lack of clarity is sometimes a device to mask the fact that the conclusions sought could not be arrived at by logical means. If a philosophic scheme starts with false premises, and has its conclusions already fixed for it, then its exponents can only give a comprehensive coverage of relevant subjects by avoiding any implication of the fact that there are no logical links between the basic principles and the answers finally arrived at. Therefore, the system must actively avoid using logic.

The lack of scientific rigour in Marx's work is more understandable, partly because of the lower standards of nineteenth century academic writings, sociology and economics both being in their infancy, and partly because of the pervasive influence of Hegel. But this is not to say that

---

1. Shlomo Avineri   *The Social and Political Thought of Karl Marx*, Cambridge University Press.

Marx was a Hegelian, or that his attitudes were similar to Hegel's; it is simply the method, and a few principles that they shared in common. Hegel was quite willing to act as court philosopher to Friedrich Wilhelm III of Prussia—Engels describes his system as being *"raised, as it were, to the rank of a Royal Prussian philosophy of state."*[1] Hegel's concept of society developing in accordance with the progress of the 'Ideals' led to the belief that the society existing at any given time was the best possible that could exist. The oppressive regime of Prussia was historically justified; if it existed, it was rational; and if it was rational, then it was acceptable. Hegel also believed that the task of philosophy was to explain past events, not to predict future ones.

Marx however was motivated by idealism in the modern sense of the word—altruism. There is a genuine feeling of anger in some of his writings, particularly in *Capital*; anger at the injustices of society, at the poverty that existed, and at the capitalists who allowed the poverty and oppression to continue. His sense of morality is rarely matched by modern Marxists, who decry the power wielded by capitalists, but look forward to the day when communists can wield the power instead. Lastly, Marx believed that the task of philosophy was not to study the past, but to predict the future; not to explain society, but to help change it.

Because of the similarities with Hegel's philosophy, and the importance of the differences, Marx no doubt felt it was necessary to stress the materialist stance of his views. But this emphasis is only of value while Hegel's views remain popular, and the distinction or comparison is being made with a current ideology. But Hegel's views no longer have anything like the popularity they enjoyed in the nineteenth century; in fact, one could say that as far as generally

1. F. Engels *Ludwig Feuerbach and the End of Classical German Philosophy.*

accepted philosophies went, Hegel was a dead duck. And there is no point in distinguishing between one's own philosophy and another one, when the second has virtually no adherents.

Marx may have had reason, but there is no value now in emphasising the difference, as Cornforth does, devoting an entire chapter just to materialism. Even if it was still valid there would be little point in stressing the distinctions between it and idealism, unless one was tracing their historical development, because one cannot meaningfully claim greater validity for one's own theory in comparison with a non-valid theory. Equally, one cannot use the faults of a non-valid theory to prove the accuracy of one's own beliefs; to claim that one's theory explains more, or predicts more accurately, then a theory which explains or predicts nothing, is a poor claim. But it is only Marxists who make any mention of idealism; everyone else, in related fields of study—those who are the modern Marxists *real* philosophical opponents—from existentialists to Chicago monetarists, have dumped idealism in the trash-can of history. Marxists are continuing to compare idealism with materialism, presumably because it is their traditional opponent, but they are only keeping it alive in order to shoot it down. But it is surely a hollow victory, and one that implies nothing about the validity of Marxism.

But supposing we take materialism as no more than the philosophy of Marxism, rather than its method, does it then have any value? Certainly, if the philosophy is not valid, it need not necessarily invalidate the method, but if the method were invalid then it would undeniably invalidate the results. one cannot get accurate results from an inaccurate method. But if materialism is merely the philosophy, then it does no harm to the truth or claims of Marxism as a science. But on the other hand, it does not add anything to the truth of Marxism.

So what is the investigative process used? The answer must be, dialectics. As stated in the previous chapter, Hegel developed dialectics in opposition to Kant, saying that one should not worry about the contradictions in a theory, because they are the basis of scientific development, the means by which the next stage of truth is discovered. Dialectics works as follows; first a thesis is proposed, its opponents point out its faults, and bring out their opposing theory, the antithesis; finally comes the synthesis, a combination of the two, with the best elements of each.

Thus, dialectics is a logic-based system of analysis that operates by comparing two opposing systems, locating their internal contradictions, and items where one theory conflicts with the other, identifying similarities, removing the unacceptable or irrational elements, and creating a new theory from what is left of the old ones. To be usable as a tool of investigation it must be capable of two separate stages; first, assuming we have only one theory to analyse, it must be able to generate an opposing theory. Second, it must be able to take two conflicting theories—one of which may be its own creation—and putting together one comprehensive theory from their components.

To do this, it must have rules and guidelines; these are essential for identifying the internal inconsistencies, and for assessing, where two theorems conflict with one another, which of them is correct. Guidelines or general principles would also be necessary in locating and phrasing the antithesis, and in locating the synthesis. For any given thesis, the antithesis posed against it must be suited to drawing out the good and bad points of the original. One could not compare communism to Euclidean geometry, or to Copernican astronomy, or to Milton Friedman's monetarist ideas on inflation; it would have to be compared with a similar theory on the construction of society. To take a practical example, Isaac Newton believed that light was made up of tiny particles; his antagonist, Christian Huygens, believed it was a wave form; each one of them had evidence to support their view, and when the issue was finally resolved it was discovered that light was comprised of particles—travelling in a wave motion.

Having obtained one's thesis and antithesis, further rules are necessary for determining which are the correct components in each, and how the synthesis should be constructed. The conflict between Newton and Huygens was based—and resolved—on empirical data; it is rare that any social scientist can offer an actual example of what the ideal social system should, and certainly Marx was not able to do this. The claim would be that using historical and dialectical laws, Marx was able to determine the correct social structure; in other words, knowing the structure and behaviour of capitalism, he was able to discover the ideal for communism.

In any verbal logic system, the way each proposition is phrased is essential to the accuracy of the results; absolute precision is vital. For example, if the thesis is—'All swans are white'—should the antithesis be—no swans are white, all swans are non-white, all swans are black, not all swans are white, all non-swans are white, or all non-swans are black? From a very simple statement we can generate six separate opposites. The correct answer to the question would be, not all swans are white; at least, this is factually correct; but that does not necessarily mean that it is the proper formulation for an antithesis. In normal use one presumably does not know what the *correct* answer is, as that is the synthesis, the final stage.

But if one were formulating an opposite for an antithesis, would one be able to generalise from the answer given, and say that if the thesis is—'All items in category A are also in category B', is the antithesis, 'Not all items in category A are also in category B'. And having run into so much trouble formulating an opposite from a simple statement, consider the prblems we could have with ideas and objects. The opposite of hot is cold, correct? But what is the opposite of warm? Or to be more precise, what is the opposite of 60°? What is the opposite of Neville Chamberlain, umbrella, piano, die-cast stamping foundry, ferret, or capitalism?

In fact, should the antithesis be the opposite—within existing knowledge—of the thesis? Or should it merely be a different, but related theorem? The problems of construction remain the same as before; what are the rules, how does one create, construct, and phrase the antithesis? Hegel does not go into details, nor does he formulate rules of logic for dialectics, but without rules it is impossible to use them in any way.

To take a practical example, if capitalism is our thesis, should we state it to be—a system in which the means of production are owned privately by a minority, the means being operated to maximise profit regardless of general welfare? If this is our thesis, then the antithesis could be—a system in which the means of production are owned socially by the majority, and these means are operated to maximise general welfare regardless of profit. This antithesis looks remarkably like the dictatorship of the proletariat, and could even be a description of the ultimate communist society. But this does not necessarily confirm Marx's use of dialectics, because this particular antithesis was only realised because of the way in which the thesis was phrased. If the thesis was stated in different terms, one would arrive at a different antithesis.

Supposing we state instead that capitalism is—a system in which the wealth and the means of production are owned by the smallest possible number of people, and an excessive proportion of the incomes derived from ownership are transferred to that group. The antithesis could then be—a system in which the wealth and means of production are owned by the greatest possible number of people, and a reasonable proportion of the incomes derived from ownership are transferred to the owning group. Now we have a definition which could be of some form of communism, but equally could apply to a small business economy, with the ownership of a multitude of small firms shared equally throughout the working population.

Obviously, the formulation of the thesis must be absolutely comprehensive, so that when the antithesis is generated from it, there is no doubt on any aspect of it. The second stage of the dialectical triad should appear in such precise terms that every part of its real-life functioning is clear and unambiguous. Because if the logical processes are such that precision is lost in going from the first stage to the second stage, then even more will be lost in going to the final stage. But even if the accuracy is only lost in generating the antithesis, we still have the fact that if the second phase is incorrect, the final synthesis will also be incorrect.

Synthesis should also be the next stage for our two examples, but each of the two antitheses is complete in itself, and as a general form would be acceptable to its supporters as it stands. Not only that, but in the latter example the use of dialectics has generated an antithesis which is a form of capitalism, and should we wish to develop a synthesis— which by definition is a combination of the best parts of the previous two stages—then it will be a capitalist synthesis. The synthesis can only contain what is in the preceding stages, therefore we have the paradox that the Marxist method can lead to decidedly non-Marxist conclusions.

And if it is sometimes possible to generate a correct and final answer directly from the thesis, as the above examples could indicate, it means that one is actually going straight from thesis to synthesis. And it would seem that this is what Marx did, his argument leading immediately from capitalism to communism, with no intermediate stage. It might be argued that that is exactly what the dictatorship of the proletariat is—but it is not; it is an intermediate stage of social development, but not a stage in a sequence of logic. It has been described as having elements of both capitalism and communism, so if we were placed at any stage of the dialectical triad, it should be the synthesis. The fact remains that Marx did not follow the full, three part process.

And if it were possible to eliminate the antithesis from the process, what we are left with is—thesis, with faults in it, discover what the faults are and create new theory. In other words, exactly what any scientist does when investigating an imperfect theory. One simply deduces what is wrong in the present theory, what parts of it give incorrect answers, or unsatisfactory functioning, deduces what needs to be changed, and calculates what the system will be like after the changes. And if the middle stage is redundant, the triad itself is valueless; it is only the antithesis which makes the dialectical process distinctive; it is the extra stage which distinguishes dialectics from conventional reasoning, and is effectively half of the final synthesis. Eliminating the antithesis invalidates dialectics in its entirety.

Although it is a fault that no rules are given, if they *were* given they would have to include rules for locating the internal contradictions of the thesis; this would be an absolute minimum considering the description of dialectics. Contradictions between the theory and empirical facts can be eliminated in the normal routine; if internal contradictions can be removed as well, then one can develop an accurate theory directly from the thesis. In other words, pass directly from thesis to synthesis. And in doing so, invalidate dialectics.

To return to the two-stage process that Marx appeared to follow, if we take capitalism as the thesis, and communism as the antithesis, then there must inevitably be a synthesis. Marx's work is simply the second stage in the triad, and the ideal society must then be a combination of the two stages existing now. Again, the problem of rules crops up, but instead of trying to define an opposite or opposing theory, we now have to compare the two theories to locate their contradictions, and form a third. But what are the rules? If the first phase of the process has created the opposite of the thesis in every way, the two will contradict one another out of existence. If the thesis were—'All swans are white', and the antithesis were—'No non-swans are black', then removing the conflicting statements leaves nothing for a synthesis. If instead we take a partial opposite—'Some swans are black', then the synthesis could be—'Not all swans are white'.

If instead the two ideologies are taken as being opposite in their general characteristics, a synthesis could be sought with the best of both, but without necessarily eliminating contradictions, or keeping elements that exist in both, then we can create virtually what we want. This introduces yet another failing of dialectics—in the absence of rules anything can be created, and anything can be proved—given the poor quality of logic that is accepted.

By removing the internal contradictions of capitalism—the class system, and the enormous concentrations of wealth and power—and the contradictions of communism—the absolute power of the state—the third stage can be formulated as a system with great social mobility, widely distributed wealth, and a state with only minimal power. Equality of wealth implies dispersed ownership—a small business economy—and a high degree of social mobility means no fixed class structure. Again, the synthesis has a non-Marxist nature. But the crucial point is that Marx's system was only a second stage; if the dialectical process is an inevitable law, then Marxism is invalidated; if communism is held to be the final stage, then dialectics is erroneous.

As mentioned in the previous chapter, these are Hegel's dialectics, and Marx is not personally responsible for them; but he accepted and adopted them as they stood, making only the philosophical change from idealism to materialism. Neither he nor Engels laid out any detailed rules, although both referred to the rules on occasion. As stated earlier, it is a logic-based system— *"formal logic is primarily a method of arriving at new results, of advancing from the known to the unknown—and dialectics is the same, only much more eminently so . . ."*[1] If this were correct, the rules of dialectics should either be more precise than those of formal logic, or else in some way more true. Neither of these possibilities seems likely, or even credible, but at least Engels could have stated the rules, to justify the comparison with logic.

He does list some of them however, saying that *"they can be reduced in the main to three: The law of the transformation of quantity into quality and vice versa; The law of the interpenetration of opposites; The law of the negation of the negation."*[2] But he does no more than name the laws; he does not specify what events they affect, or in what way, or under what conditions. And he goes on to say that *"we cannot go into the inner interconnection of these laws with one another."*[3]

Examples are given of the operation of these laws at various points in the writings of Marx and Engels, but no precise formulations are given. *"We gave there one of the best known examples—that of the change of the aggregate states of water, which under normal atmospheric pressure changes at 0°C from the liquid into the solid state, and at 100°C from the liquid into the gaseous state, so that at both these turning points the merely quantitative change of*

1. F. Engels *Anti-Duhring.*
2. Engels *Dialectics of Nature.*
3. Engels, op. cit.

temperature brings about a qualitative change in the condition of the water.''[1]

A typical case of the negation of the negation occurs when *"a grain of barley meets with conditions which are normal for it, if it falls on suitable soil . . . it germinates; the grain as such ceases to exist, it is negated, and in its place appears the plant which has arisen from it, the negation of the grain. (The plant) grows, flowers, is fertilized and finally once more produces grain of barley . . .''*[2]

But are these laws universal? If so, then presumably all instances of communism—the negation of capitalism—will also be negated, and such societies will return to capitalism thus bringing about the negation of the negation. If the laws are not universal then Engels—or Marx—should have stated exactly what they apply to, and which type of event they do not apply to. And there do not seem to be even examples to explain Engels' second law.

In fact, they are not even entitled to the name, 'laws'. A scientific law does not merely state that under specified conditions a predicted result will occur from a given event; such laws also state why things happen as they do. The explanation may not be stated in the law, but any scientist would be able to show why events must occur in a particular way. In the case of the laws of dialectics, Engels should not merely have stated what the laws applied to, and under what conditions they operated—he should also have explained and proved what it is that universally impels things to follow these laws.

For example, he should not only have explained why water boils, and what it is doing at the moment of boiling; he should also have demonstrated and proved the separate dialectical law which impels all substances—water, oil, steel,

1. Engels *Anti-Duhring.*
2. Engels, op cit.

mercury, helium—to change their form when their temperature is raised or lowered beyond a certain point. Or else the law should prove why all changes of quantity must, universally and automatically, result in a change of quality. Similarly, are all negations followed by a negation of the negation? Engels should have specified whether it was universal or not, if it was not universal he should have stated what it did apply to, and in either case he should have made quite clear what conditions applied. Finally, he should have proved that certain types of negation must inevitably be followed by a further negation.

At no time does Engels give any evidence of the universal nature of the laws, indeed, it is hard to see them as laws at all; it is simply that some types of event can be classified in a certain way. The classification is purely arbitrary, the examples are unrelated, and no proof whatsoever is given for the laws. One could equally say that lots of things that move tend to stop—cars, people, antelopes, and tidal waves; this shows (or could show, given just a little willingness to believe anything whatsoever) the law of negation of motion. Sometimes—as with pneumatic drills, sewing machines, or dogs' teeth sinking into postmens' ankles—the movement stops, reverses, then returns; this could be the law of cyclic motion.

The above laws are just as valid as those put forward by Engels; they are nonsense, but they describe certain categories of action. The movements, processes, or developments that they could refer to are totally unrelated. They are instigated by different scientific, biological, mechanical, or geophysical laws; but they are not influenced by laws that exist above the known rules of science.

But putting aside the question of validity, what do the laws refer to; are they the means of generating an antithesis from a thesis? The phrasing and the examples given imply that they are laws of development rather than of logic, they would perhaps describe historical progress rather than analyse a social system. Indeed, Engels does say that *"they are nothing but the most general laws of these two aspects* (Engels refers to nature and human society) *of historical development."*[1] But are they also the laws of dialectical analysis? Engels offers no answer; one can only presume that they are. But if these are the laws of dialectics, then there are no laws at all. They could be used after the event to prove anything, but in analysing before the event—prediction— they prove nothing.

But perhaps Marxist science has progressed in the last hundred years, and the dialectics of Hegel, Marx, and Engels has been replaced by something more modern, more precise. Or perhaps they have simply been rejected. Lichtheim says that Marxist socialists have *"inherited"* those aspects of Hegel's work that Marx incorporated into his own; by implication he is including dialectics as part of the Marxist tradition. And Cornforth devotes a chapter to dialectics, quoting mainly from the works of Engels. There is no sign of any rejection of Engels' laws, nor of their being replaced by more suitable forms. Marxism is still fixed firmly in the nineteenth century.

The final conclusion can only be that the scientific basis of Marxism is hopelessly out of date. Its philosophy is no more than a historical curiosity, while its method is just a collection of generalisations concerning totally unrelated phenomena. There is even the contradiction that if dialectics is correct, then Marx's social system is wrong; but if communism is valid, then all the Marxist claims of scientific status are wrong.

But it is not merely unscientific—it also gives a very poor definition of the type of society we should aim for. The

1. F. Engels *Dialectics of Nature.*

Marxist utopia is one of centralisation and state power, and when put into practice there is the possibility that it will result in the worst kind of tyranny. This alone is reason enough to justify the most intense scrutiny of Marxism. Every person who accepts the claims of Marxism is taking his country, his political system, that much closer to dictatorship. Admittedly, not all communist countries are tyrannies, but there are enough of them to justify caution and criticism.

The practical aspect of Marxism which most deserves critical analysis is the dictatorship of the proletariat; this will be examined in the next chapter.

3

One-Way System

The Transitional Phase

The function of society is to benefit the individual, the member of society. It may be seen as having other functions, but its central purpose must be to look after the benefit of the individual—each and every individual. The state's policies may cover health, housing, education, justice, foreign aid, and grants to cultural organisations. Some policies may benefit all members, while others help only one particular group. But the guiding principle must be—the greatest possible good for the greatest possible number.

Each society is an aritificial construct which, given the choice, people become or remain part of for the advantages they will receive. And if a given society offers no advantages, or gives less than could be offered, then it is failing in its purpose. The people should then have the right and the ability to remove from office those of the government who support incorrect policies. Equally, they should have the right to leave their country, should they regard that as the only practical alternative.

If the system fails its members, either because its basic structure is faulty, or because the policies selected by its ruler are unsuitable, then that society must be open to change, the rulers must be willing to choose alternative policies, and if not, they must be subject to dismissal by the electorate. As these conditions supposedly apply to the capitalist democracies, then we in the west should have an ideal society. But in many of the modern western democracies something is very obviously wrong—yet nothing is done. There is extensive property, hideous slums, rising crime rates, and gross inequalities of wealth and income. And nothing is done.

To some people this seems like an inherent fault in democracy; the majority vote for the policies and government that they want, and if any minority group does not get fair treatment, its just unfortunate. The government is voted in by the majority, and the only groups that they have to concern themselves with are the ones who give them power. The majority want their interests looked after, and the politicians want office. This selfishness, which seems to be a common fault in democracies, brings us to one of the most crucial objections to capitalism, and the reason why many people see communism as being morally superior. The fact is that capitalism is implicitly based on selfishness, because the principle of self-interest is a fundamental part of the theory behind capitalism. And all too often the most glaring faults of capitalist society are the direct result of the selfishness of one sector or another.

In traditional market theory every participant is motivated by a self-interest; the consumer seeks the lowest possible prices, and the manufacturer seeks the highest prices obtainable and the highest profits he can get. Self-interest is the psychological lynch-pin, the only motive recognised in economics. In the words of the Communist Manifesto, bourgeois economics *"has left remaining no other nexus between man and the man than naked self-interest, than callous 'cash payment'. It has drowned the most heavenly ecstasies of religious fervour, of chivalrous enthusiasm, of philistine sentimentalism, in the icy water of egotistical calculation. It has resolved personal worth into exchange value.''*[1]

Communism operates on a completely different basis; here, the guiding principle is welfare. The sole purpose and motive of communist society is the well-being of its citizens. In the ultimate phase of communism the state is dissolved, and the members of society, all being equal, will be free to pursue their maximum welfare without impinging on the needs of others.

But before the ultimate phase is achieved, there is a transitional phase, sometimes known as socialism or the lower phase of communism. *"Between capitalist and communist society lies the period of the revolutionary transformation of the one into the other. There corresponds to this also a political transition period in which the state can be nothing but the revolutionary dictatorship of the proletariat.''*[2] In the transitional phase the state will still exist, but it will allocate goods and services according to need; from each according to his ability, to each according to his need. Welfare will still be the primary consideration, but the means of maximising this will be decided by the state.

But what is communism, and what is the dictatorship of the proletariat? Before answering these questions in detail I must once again mention Cornforth's accusation against Popper, that Popper attacked not what Marxism is, but what he said Marxism is. It was a false accusation, but in the hope that no Marxist can correctly accuse the present writer of misrepresentation, I shall quote where possible from the works of Marx, Engels, Lenin, and Bebel. August Bebel may not be a well-known name in the annals of communism, but he was a contemporary and correspondent of both Marx and Engels, one of the five people to whom Marx sent a draft copy of the *Critique of the Gotha Programme*, and one of the co-founders of the Social Democratic Worker Party.

1. Marx and Engels   *The Manifesto of the Communist Party.*
2. Marx   *Critique of the Gotha Programme.*

With Marx and Engels, he played a leading role in running the party's paper, and he also worked with them on the German Worker Association's paper. And at the International Congress of 1903, when the 'revisionist', Bernstein, put forward the idea that change could occur gradually, without a revolution, it was a group led by Bebel that held the Congress to the accepted revolutionary view.

Hopefully, the following will present a reasonably accurate picture of Marxist theory as it was at the end of the nineteenth century, and the beginning of the twentieth. In nearly every case it will also be a valid picture of contemporary Marxism.

Although the ideology is named communism, it is the lower phase, the dictatorship of the proletariat, which is the immediate goal of Marxists. It is this phase which receives most attention in Marxist literature, and at which existing Marxist societies are still fixed. So it is this phase which deserves the most careful analysis.

In the transitional phase the workers take control of the reins of state to transfer ownership of the means of production, and so abolish the inequalities that existed under the old regime. The theory states that society will then be run for the benefit of all; at least in theory. But in virtually all the literature the emphasis is placed on the working class. For example, *"the first step in the revolution of the working class, is to raise the proletariat to the position of ruling class, to win the battle of democracy"*.[1]   It is one thing to state that under the new system neither the working class nor any other social class will be oppressed; it is even reasonable to emphasise the freedom of the working class from oppression, because it is they who are most harshly treated. But it is quite another thing to say that the workers must be placed in the same position, and with the same

1. Marx and Engels   *Manifesto of the Communist Party.*

power, as the rulers of the old system.

It implies that the power wielded under the old regime was perfectly valid and justified; the only things wrong are that it was not wielded by the working class—and that it was used against the working class. But it is morally acceptable for the proletariat to use power—and perhaps violence—against the bourgeoisie. What was wrong with the old system was not the existence of great power, but the identity of the people who held it. Government by a small group of aristocrats is wrong; but government by a small group of workers is fine. As Lord Thomson of Fleet said, *"I think monopoly in anything is a bad thing for the public. I like it for myself . . ."* Great power is a very bad thing—in your hands—but if I have it, then its alright.

Also, the revolution is always stated in terms of political control, taking over the government. It has always been made clear that the real source of power is wealth, and that the real location of power is in the means of production. Yet when seeking a transfer of power Marxists talk about taking over the political system; the economy comes as a secondary consideration. There has been no thorough study of the reasoning behind this, and the implications are, first, that Marxists do not completely understand the system—which they should, if they have any real hope of changing it. Second, that the real goal of Marxism is political power; what comes after that is subsidiary, the power is wanted for itself.

Because the intended state was considered to be so radically different from existing society, Marx decreed that the state had to be made more powerful to enable it to effect the changes needed to create the ideal society. Thus we have the interesting paradox that to create a society in which the state will wither away, the state is strengthened and enlarged. The new socialist state will be taking over all control, both political and economic, and so must acquire additional powers to control and re-educate the old bourgeoisie.

The old capitalist class would still be extremely powerful, and their knowledge of *"state, military and economic administration gives them a superiority, and a very great superiority, so that their importance is incomparably greater than their numerical proportion among the population would warrant"*.[1] Because of this power held by the bourgeoisie, *"they can (and must) be re-moulded and re-educated only by very prolonged, slow, cautious organizational work"*.[2] As long as the old establishment remains in existence, it is a threat, not only because of its power, but also because it is part of *"the forces and traditions of the old society. The force of habit of millions and tens of millions is a most terrible force"*.[3] If the state lacked sufficient power, the old capitalist ways would return, aided by the power of the bourgeoisie, and the habits and traditions of the working class.

"The class of exploiters, the landlords and capitalists, has not disappeared and cannot disappear all at once under the dictatorship of the proletariat. The exploiters have been smashed, but not destroyed. They still have an international base in the form of international capital, a branch of which they represent. They still retain a part of certain means of production, they still have money, they still have vast social connections. Just because they have been defeated, their energy of resistance has increased a hundred-and thousand-fold".[4]

1. V.I. Lenin   *Economics and Politics in the Dictatorship of the Proletariat.*
2. Lenin   *'Left-Wing' Communism.*
3. Lenin, op. cit.
4. Lenin   *Economics and Politics.*

To combat this power, to prevent the corruption of the proletariat, and to prevent relapses, the *"strictest centralisation and discipline are required within the political party of the proletariat"*.[1] To eliminate the problems of corruption, profiteering, and so on *"requires time and requires* an iron hand"[2] (emphasis in original). The new state must *"retain power sufficiently to suppress completely all the exploiters as well as all the elements of disintegration."*[3]

So to transfer power from the old bourgeoisie to the new state requires power of a particularly potent and unusual sort. It must be potent in order that it may effectively combat the residual power of the old capitalist class with their money and social connections. It must be capable of forcing capitalists to behave in the approved maner, regardless of the residual influence wielded by the capitalists.

And it would be unusual in that many members of the old administration would have to stay in office—this is clear from Lenin's complain regarding their disproportionate power, and from the simple fact that one cannot remove a complete administrative system overnight. There must be a modest interregnum of sorts, while the old hands tell the new boys where the tea is kept, what categories of information are on file, how to obtain fast access to specific items of information, and so on.

At least some of the members of the old administration, and most of the capitalists, would be noticeably lacking in sympathy for the new regime. So the new state must be able to force the executive classes to carry on working for a system that they do not like or approve of. Much of this ability to force people to work comes from the fact that the state controls all sources of income, that the state owns all

1. Lenin *'Left-Wing' Communism.*
2. Lenin *The Immediate Tasks of the Soviet Government.*
3. Lenin, op. cit.

means of production, and therefore, all sources of employment. And obviously, the old guard can perform their jobs with apparent efficiency, while at the same time trying to unbalance and dislocate the system.

A bureaucrat can carefully examine the same file a dozen times, or re-file all important documents at the back of the 'miscellaneous' section. He can pass on all decisions to other departments and ministries, until even the most simple task gets bogged down in correspondence between six ministries and three local authorities. And the capitalist can order a million tons of coal for his factory when he actually needs ten million; or order soldering equipment when he really needs welding tackle. Or he can ship the occasional consignment of finished goods to the wrong town.

To combat this sort of behaviour the state must have the means to monitor the efficiency of the administrators—especially those running the factories—and must find some way to force them to work properly. The ex-owners of the factories would in the past have been running them purely out of self-interest, but because of that they would presumably have sought to run them as efficiently as possible. Now they are running things for the state, at a comparatively low income, they no longer have any incentive to do their best; while they have every reason to resent, even hate, the new regime. Given the obviousness of the state's need to monitor efficiency and output, it could be assumed that the capitalists would seek some way of giving the appearance of efficiency without the reality. Thus, the state's monitoring system must be effective, fool-proof, and discreet; perhaps even undercover. And so one has the beginnings of a secret police.

There is also the possibility of conspiracies between individuals; secret arrangements to hide evidence of mismanagement, use of their 'vast social connections', and perhaps even attempts to bring back to old system. So the state must also be able to discreetly observe the private behaviour of the old guard. It must of course have the power to punish offenders—but without the threat of imprisonment, for this would negate the whole purpose of leaving the old administrators free, to smooth the transfer of government and ownership. And those whose wealth has been confiscated, and whose extortionate incomes have beeen reduced to a more modest level, cannot be reasonably expect to pay large fines.

So occasionally, different methods of punishment will be sought—and used. It should be no surprise if, in the interim period in some countries, methods of punishment are used that are harsher than would be considered acceptable under normal conditions. It is often a chaotic period, with no fixed legel or judicial system, no clear chain of command, and perhaps no clearly specified authorities. Under such conditions, anyone working for the quasi-police org-anisation could go to a powerful government official, and ask for the authority to make whatever changes were necessary—to convert a quasi-police force into a powerful secret police. The uncertainty of such periods allows all sorts of people to rise to the top—but usually the worst sorts.

In addition to members of the old regime, there will be thousands, perhaps millions of people who may or may not have received any great share of the benefits under the old system, but still believe in its principles, and would prefer to live under its rule. This could be true even of those actually exploited by their previous employers; but because they were used to it, and had adapted to it, they regret its passing. The *"forces and traditions of the old society"* do not die easily. Its working class sympathisers, and the old bourgeoisie, must all be re-educated; and this is not a process they will volunteer for.

A person's beliefs are part of his or her character, and are not something to be shed lightly. On the surface there are beliefs like, 'I think it might rain tomorrow' or 'I think my next-door-neighbour is a busdriver', and such beliefs can be shed with no great difficulty. But sometimes people believe in the system they work for, or their monarch, or their government, with a fervour that denies rational analysis. They are usually beliefs that people have grown up with, have taken for granted all their lives, and fit in with a whole series of related beliefs. If capitalism is necessary, then the division of labour is necessary—so for each individual worker the job that he does is part of his unique contribution to society. To attack the validity of capitalism is to threaten his identity; to remove the capitalist system is an all-out assault on his identity.

So in addition to its new courses in 'adult education', the state must have the means of forcing people to take such courses, to acquire beliefs that are alien to them. They must not only be forced to learn the new ideology; they must in the interim be forced to act on it.

From its idealistic position of working for the welfare of its people, as their servant, the theorists of the socialist state have now adopted the role of teacher. The state knows what is right, and what the people must believe, and it will deploy its considerable resources to making sure that they do believe what they are supposed to. Thus, even truth is centralised. The state is the arbiter of the type of economy that is needed, the sort of policies needed, and by implication, what must be done to maximise welfare. So the state, and only the state, knows what its people want. From welfare to paternalism in one easy step.

The state will tell the people what to believe, using indoctrination courses, government controlled press and media, and slanted news censorship. And when control of education and the media is ideologically acceptable, then who is to say when it is no longer practically necessary? Once it exists it creates its own momentum and its own justification. If any workers have the temerity to criticise the government for not producing enough food or housing, then obviously they are failing to appreciate the heroic efforts of the socialist leadership, in the face of daunting, overwhelming, and etc. So instead of examining the truth or otherwise of the workers' criticisms, the state-owned press will issue a broadside against ill-informed critics, or reactionary saboteurs. It is so much easier to do. When one has total power, one need not justify one's actions to anybody.

So the new proletarian state has powers that are not usually part of the apparatus of a capitalist democracy. Not that the western nations are anywhere near perfect; in America, blacks were not allowed to vote in some states until quite recently, while in Germany, anyone suspected of being sympathetic to communism, or in any way disloyal to the German state, is not allowed to hold a government job— they are *Berufsverbot*—profession forbidden.

But the faults of democracy do not prove the truth of communism. And the communist state has some remarkable powers, no matter who one compares it to. But is such a state really necessary? In strict Marxist terms it is. Marx stated that *"the class struggle necessarily leads to the dictatorship of the proletariat"*. Not that it might lead, or will probably lead, but that it necessarily leads. The existence of the class struggle is basic to Marxism, therefore the intermediate dictatorship is also. *"Only he is a Marxist who extends the recognition of the class struggle to the recognition of the dictatorship of the proletariat. This is what constitutes the most profound difference between the Marxist and the ordinary petty (as well as big) bourgeois. This is the touchstone on which the real understanding and recognition of Marxism is to be tested."*[1]

1. V.I. Lenin   *The State and Revolution.*

Thus, it is a crucial aspect of Marxist theory. It is inevitable, and even though it is only the transitional state, belief in it is essential if one is to be a Marxist. But is it necessary in practice? Is it logically necessary? To take the logic first, from this point of view the whole exercise seems rather pointless. If one is aiming for an ideal state, then the transitional state should be of minor concern; if there is one at all. The introduction of an extra phase into the theory complicates things, and perhaps is an unnecessary complication. Marx should have started out with the basic theory of the communist state—its aims, its purpose, its general structure, its economic policies, and so on. Then he should have proved that a direct change was not possible—and why it was not. Then he should have gone into details regarding the transitional phase. Marx did not prove any of these three items, but our concern right now is that he failed to prove the necessity of the transitional phase.

But even assuming that an extra phase is necessary, why should it be of this particular type? The objection to the old system was that capitalists used their economic and political power to control society and exploit the workers. So the transitional phase puts the workers in full economic and political control; but not all the workers; by definition, a centralised society cannot be rulled co-operatively or jointly, therefore, only a small group of workers will actually form the government. If centralisation of control is the objection to capitalism, there is nothing to be gained by replacing one centralised system with another. If exploitation is the main complaint, there is no advantage in removing one set of exploiters, and then putting a different set of people in the same seat of power, still able to continue the exploitation.

The fact is that centralisation of power means that one small group of people are the rulers, and removing every individual in that group, and replacing them with people from a different social class, changes nothing. With any given political system, the power to exploit is constant; the identity of the ruling group has no effect on the level of opportunity. For the workers' group to be effective rulers, they must stay in office long enough to get the hang of things; which would also be long enough to learn the perks and privileges of power. And long enough for some of them to learn how to use that power, and the uncertainty of the interim period, to ensure that their stay in office lasts as long as they want it to. Rule by the workers becomes rule by individuals who had a working-class background.

Thus, Marx's suggested transformation of the system becomes only a nominal change in control. But perhaps his real concern was with the moral right to govern. That is, that capitalists do not have the moral right to rule the workers. Citizens should be governed by their peers, by people with a similar background, with an understanding of everyday problems; so workers should be ruled by workers. But because society is made up of different classes, it is not possible for everyone to be governed by their peers; the best compromise is a government that is answerable to the people, and in touch with their needs.

But even though there is no logical reason why the dictatorship of the proletariat should be an essential stage, there are reasons why Marx should have considered it necessary at the time; and equally, reasons why Marx would have thought a violent revolution to be required. Throughout Europe political power—the right to vote—was dependent solely on one's wealth. In Prussia there was a three class voting system, with the rich in the first class, civil servants or administrators in the second or third class, and the workers with no vote at all. In England, voting had been the sole prerogative of the upper classes since 1295, and it was not until the reform of 1832 that even the middle classes got the right to vote. In France, out of a population of 36 million, only 240,000 people had the right to vote.

In the words of Rousseau, *"Man was born free, but everywhere he is in chains."* The governments of that time were the ones put in, and kept in office, by the rich—the people with the least intention of making any changes. The people with the most need to create change were the poor, the workers, the disenfrancished lower orders.

The chains that bound the workers was their poverty— which forced them to accept whatever wages were offered; which wasn't much. The workers were exploited to a degree that was barbaric, so that costs could be kept low, and profits kept high—to provide more money for more factories, and hence, more exploitation. Wages were not only pitifully low, they were kept low by legislation; employers were not allowed to pay above a certain fixed level. It was not until 1813 that the maximum wage laws were repealed, not that wages shot up after that, nor would anyone with a vote want them to. In 1874 an article in The Economist observed that wages were not taking a greater slice of the national income than they had earlier in the century; and it was noted, there was no reason why wages should grow. Workers had no automatic right to any particular amount of income, and certainly no right to a steadily increasing income.

Paying low wages was considered quite justified; it was good for the country. The attitude behind this was summed up by a writer named Arthur Young, who in 1771 said, *"Everyone but an idiot knows that the lower classes must be kept poor or they will never be industrious."* So Britain became the workshop of the world—at the expense of the working class.

Lacking money, they of course lacked influence as well. Merchants, landowners, and businessmen were the ones with money, and the political influence to instigate what Marx described as *"savage legislation."* Obviously the workers were also unable to form their own companies or factories, or in any way make themselves independent of the system. Money makes money—but when one has the bare minimum for survival, one has no chance of becoming rich. Therefore one has no way of changing things.

Thus, at the time that Marx was writing, a revolution followed by a dictatorship of the proletariat was perhaps the only conceivable way of producing change. The only form of power that the workers had was sheer numbers—and violence. *"The supersession of the bourgeois state by the proletarian state is impossible without a violent revolution."*[1] And the violent overthrow of an established regime must be followed by a period of adjustment, while the old guard and their sympathisers get used to the idea that an irreversible change has occurred, and the new rulers learn how to run things.

But the transitional phase is only necessary if a violent method of change is the only possibility. If reform can be introduced gradually, then the whole period of transformation is also a time for readjustment; people can get used to the changing scheme of things while it actually occurs. Thus, if reform is possible, then a violent revolution is not necessary; and so, the dictatorship of the proletariat becomes redundant.

And a lot has happened in the 130 years since Marx started writing, including many things which Marx should have seen and allowed for in his theories. The Whig government obtained office in 1830, mainly because of its promises of reform; and when the 1831 Reform Bill was thrown out by the House of Lords, riots followed, and many feared that a violent revolution was actually at hand. This pressure led to the Reform Bill of 1832 which ended a continuous reign of over 550 years of upper-class-only voting, and gave the franchise to the middle classes. Admittedly, it was not until

1. V.I. Lenin, op. cit.

the Reform Act of 1867 that the urban working class were given the vote, but Marx should still have been able to take this into account; that was the year that he published the first volume of *Capital*.

And the barbaric conditions of the workers were also slowly being improved. Acts passed in 1833, '34, '40, '42, '64 and '75 extended protection to women and children working in mines and factories, as well as to chimneysweeps. Shaftesbury's act of 1842 totally forbade the employment of women and children in mines. At this time, Marx was no more than a radical journalist, unaffected by the revolutionary spirit of Paris, not yet educated by his researches at the British Museum.

Wages were also rising. The maximum wages laws that had been repealed in 1813 put an end to over 400 years of legalised exploitation, and very slowly, wages rose. Then came the boom of 1844. There was a shortage of labour because of emigration, and more significantly, the rapid expansion of the railways, but in that year wages really started to take off. There was a slight fall in the fifties, but apart from that, the middle of the century brought a continuous rise in living standards right up to the mid 70s. Just in the single decade from 1860, wages rose 20%.

All of this should have been observed and noted by Marx, with due modification to his theories. The England in which he lived and worked was undergoing a dramatic transformation. In a twenty year period the total legal supports of upper class power, and of working class poverty, were eliminated, and five hundred years of history came to an end. Marx, of all people, should have seen that the England he lived in was not the same as the country whose history he must surely have studied. It was a country undergoing an industrial revolution, and if the relations of production must adapt to the forces of production, then it follows automatically that a social revolution must also occur. If Marx's theory was correct—and on this one general point it was—then society must change. And it did.

But somehow Marx failed to take all this into account. He believed that increasing production would bring increasing exploitation; but it didn't; it created a shortage of labour, thus creating pressures to raise wages to attract labour. He assumed that the misery of the workers would increase; but it didn't; working conditions improved, and living standards rose. He thought that a violent revolution was the only possible way to create change; it but wasn't. Electoral reforms were introduced, and were slowly followed by political reforms.

As with many things, Marx changed his views on England and revolution. In a letter written in 1880 he referred to such an event as being no more than possible. He also observed that every possible concession had been wrung from the upper classes; in effect, that reform had been achieved by legal means. This reform, which had been continuing steadily for sixty years, meant that revolution was no longer inevitable; actually, it had not been inevitable since 1820, if ever, but it was not until 1880 that Marx realised this.

His failing was not merely an oversight regarding one country's practical development; it is a flaw in his whole theory. Because the crucial fact is that Marx's laws of exploitation, oppression, and revolution were based on the perceived facts of capitalist development, as drawn from the experience of England. But Marx misinterpreted all the events he saw—and perhaps ignored some events—seeing laws where there were not even tendencies, and growing oppression where actually there was reform. And if the evidence had been misinterpreted, then the empirical base for those laws was absent, and the laws themselves were untrue. They were supposed to apply universally, but they were derived wrongly, and have only proved to be universal in their inaccuracy.

But even disregarding the actual events of the nineteenth century, it was still impossible for Marx's predictions to come true. He postulated an economy of growing production, with increasing profits, levels of investment, and exploitation. With more being produced there must be higher levels of sales; and purchases of consumer goods cannot be made by workers whose wages condemn them to mere subsistence level. At some point the capitalists are obliged to raise wages in order to create a market for their goods: affluent workers are essential for a growing economy. There is no doubt that the factory owners realised this, but equally obviously, Marx did not.

But perhaps Marx saw the changes that occurred as no more than random; a slight improvement in conditions in the short term, but of no great significance on the longer historical scale. We now have the benefit of hindsight, and perhaps can see the nineteenth century in a way that Marx could not. If so, then we all have hindsight, and the excuses that can be offered for Marx cannot be accepted from modern Marxists.

Not only do we have a clear idea of the past, the present offers its own disproof of the inevitability of a communist revolution. Nowadays all adults have the vote, and political parties are no longer the private property of the rich. Admittedly, in most countries there is at least one party that is identified with the establishment, but on the other hand, there is always a non-establishment party as well. Some would even say that the Labour Party in Britain is no more than the political wing of the trade unions.

But the important fact is that the working class now have the political power to remove a party from office. Because the working class are the largest social class, it is their vote which decides who shall get into office. So if radical candidates and policies were available, and the workers wanted to vote for them, they could create an electorally inspired revolution almost overnight. Unfortunately, no established party offers genuine, practical policies for radical, long-term change, but that does not alter the fact that change *can*—in theory—be instigated by political means. All parties have to be responsive to the wishes of the people, and if the electorate stood up and said, we want this particular sort of change, the established parties would give it to them. The only reason why modern Marxists still preach revolution is the knowledge that Marxism is not acceptable at the ballot box.

Equally, a party seeking to create political change would state its policies clearly, and explain to the electorate the benefits of, and the reasoning behind, its platform. By canvassing and explaining it will inevitably attract some adherents, and hopefully, the closer its policies are to practical truth, the more votes it will get. Such a party could even be unsuccessful at the ballot box, but succeed at creating change. Whenever a minority party attracts attention, votes, or publicity, the established parties soon modify their own policies to attract fringe members of the minority group.

Change can also be created by economic means. Whereas in the early part of the nineteenth century most of the population earned only just enough for subsistence, at the present time the majority are paid sufficiently well to live in comfort, and save money. These savings could be used as the basis to create new firms, new shops, new factories; many workers could become businessmen instead of being employees, and could make themselves totally independent of the system. More important, each new company would take sales away from the big established companies.

The rich get their money from the companies they own, as shareholders, or that they control, as executives; and the companies get their money from the products they sell. And the very large incomes that some people receive are entirely dependent on the profits of the companies. There is a growing realisation that big business is not as beneficial as it claims to be, and as awareness of the defects of monopoly capitalism grows, so more and more people will turn to small firms. These small companies must inevitably take more and more sales away from the big corporations, and as their sales diminish, so will their profits, and so will the incomes of their owners. It would not be a dramatic, overnight process; companies started this year will not be panicking the executives of GEC or Shell by next year. But change would occur.

So society can be transformed gradually by political or economic means; a matter of years perhaps, which is admittedly not so dramatic as a sudden revolutionary overthrow of the established order, but quite effective. And when reform occurs gradually, there is no need for an additional period of adjustment, because the time during which the change occurs is the period of adjustment. The very fact that gradual reform is possible—regardless of the method of reform—means that the dictatorship of the proletariat is no longer necessary. The 'touchstone' of Marxism is redundant.

But assuming that it was a necessary phase, would it be transitory? For Marxism to be valid, it *must* be transitory. Its passing would have to be proven with absolute certainty; it must be swept away by historical laws that are inevitable and undeniable. But unfortunately Marx did not go into much detail on the laws which were to end the lower phase of communism. This is one of his worst oversights, but to be generous, may be one that has only become so glaringly obvious since the failure of Russia to abolish its proletariat state; becoming instead a non-transitory dictatorship.

There seem to be just two forces that will lead to the withering away of the state, and the end of the lower phase. *"The economic basis . . . is such a high stage of*

*development of communism that the antithesis between
mental and physical labour disappears, and consequently
one of the principal sources of modern social inequality
disappears . . .''*[1] The implication is that the economy will
have developed in such a way that the distinction between
mental and physical labour are no longer of great
importance to the economy, and so cease to be important
socially. Thus snobbishness and class distinctions also come
to an end, and ultimately the very idea of class itself
disappears.

No doubt the economy will still have to perform certain
distinctions, for example, it will train some people to be
plumbers, and some to be accountants. The plumber will
learn about soldered joints, water outflows, and fitting
radiators and baths; the accountant will learn about double-
entry book-keeping, Last-in, Last-out systems, and
inflation compensated accounting. To employ either one of
these in the job learnt by the other would lead to total
disaster—of one sort or another. In this sense, even in the
higher phase of communism there is still a distinction
between mental and physical labour.

But presumably it is only snobbishness that Marxists wish
to eliminate; a nice idea, but even allowing for the end of
class distinction which is supposed to come after, it bears no
resemblance to a law tht will dispose of the lower phase. It is
merely a social improvement that could occur in any
reasonably enlightened society.

The next item is that the transfer of ownership to the
state *"will inevitably result in a gigantic development of
the productive forces of human society.''*[2] The implication is that under socialism the economy will be managed
with such efficiency that its capacity will increase

1. V.I. Lenin, op. cit.
2. Lenin, op. cit.

enormously. This is a dubious proposition, but even if it were correct, it also leads to no historical law. Lenin relates it to a phrase of Marx's, of labour becoming 'life's prime want', but even in the original text there is no indication of what Marx means.

Thus, we are left with a nice idea that could happen anywhere, and a supposition that is not related to anything. For the development from capitalism to socialism Marx detailed a series of laws, leading to one inescapable conclusion. For the more important stage there is virtually nothing. There is nothing whatsoever in Marxism to prove that the dictatorship of the proletariat is transitory.

But if it is not transitional in theory, perhaps it can be in practice. But for this to be true, two conditions must be filled. First, having given absolute economic and politicial control to the chosen leaders, there must be a way of ensuring that they or their successors will relinquish it when the time comes. Second, it must be possible for the state structure to be dissolved in the way Marx postulated. Both of these conditions must be fulfilled before the ultimate phase of communism becomes practical.

The proletariat state will take over all factories and land, there will be *"Centralisation of credit in the hands of the State, by means of a national bank with State capital and an exclusive monopoly. Centralisation of the means of communication and transport in the hands of the State."*[1] In addition the state will run the education system, housing, plus the police, the army, and the judiciary. And presumably its quasi-police, its monitoring and observance system for dealing with dissidents and reactionaries. In other words, the state owns and controls virtually everything. It is possible that some people would be allowed to keep their own homes and shops, but this would be dependent on each individual leader's personal beliefs.

In theory the workers own all the resources that are taken

1. Marx and Engels *The Manifesto of the Communist Party.*

over; but they do not own anything in any meaningful sense of the word. They do not have control, or the right to dispose of their assets, or the right to keep an agreed proportion of the fruits of ownership, or even the right to decide how the assets should be operated. It is as ridiculous to say that the workers own the means of production as it is to say that a British worker who belongs to a pension scheme owns ICI. Without full possession, the right to control, and the right to operate things according to one's own opinions, there is no real ownership. The workers are just employees with illusions of grandeur.

The people who do own, in every real sense of the word, are those power, the chosen few who run the centralised state. They are the ones that decide where new factories shall be located, how the factories should be run, how much the workers will be paid, how many houses will be built to accommodate the workers, how the education system should operate—in fact, every aspect of the economy and society. 'They' control everything.

There are no indications in Marxist theory to say how many people would be in charge, but judging by existing socialist states it could be just one person; or there could be a committee of perhaps a dozen. It is even possible that the state would be run by 600 elected MPs, but this seems improbable considering the emphasis that Marx, and Marxists, place on centralisation. Regardless of the actual number, all decisions are taken by a group that is an insignificant fraction of the population in percentage terms. But the smaller the group, the smaller the range of opinions that are considered before coming to a decision.

According to Marx, the ownership structure of the economy affects the way in which the economy—and society—works. Following these principles Marx should have been able to state exactly how the economy of the transitional state should be structured in order to create the sort of system he was aiming at. He failed to do this, but it is quite obvious that as we are studying a totally centralised state, we can expect it to function in a way that is quite unlike any other system. If nothing else, all the decisions taken will have a completely arbitrary nature; and this is even if we assume that the people in command genuinely wish to do their best for their citizens. It is just not possible for one, or even a dozen persons, to have a complete understanding of every aspect of the economy, plus all the related issues of accounting, information survey techniques, the relative merits of mechanisation in every industry from automobiles to micro-chips to zinc recycling, plus exact knowledge of the specific types of machinery needed. Plus every factor and relationship in social development, from urban planning to welfare, architectural design, and even criminology. And in addition, all the special needs and characteristics of each and every town, village, farm, factory, and shop.

It is quite enough for one person to understand the general principles of society's operation, but to try to control every sector, each one with its own economic, social, and geographic peculiarities, is too much for any one person, or even a dozen persons. Should a farm in one particular region grow wheat, barley, or apples? Well, this depends on the soil, the terrain, the climate, and even the size of the farm and the availability of transport; only the farmer is really qualified to make such decisions; but he might not be allowed to. Should the trains be electric or diesel? The answer to this depends on the efficiency of the various types of locomotive available, the ease and cost at which fuel is obtained, and the terrain over which the trains will run.

There are just too many fields of expertise for the rulers to be qualified in everything, and to know to what extent and in which way local conditions must be taken into account. Therefore, they do the best they can, and base their decisions on what they believe is right; and what people belive is sometimes nothing to do with reality. Quite often they will be wrong, partly because they lack expertise, but mainly because they are just too far away from the site of the problem to understand what is really needed.

The controllers could set out general guidelines, and leave the detailed decisions to local experts, or even better, to local farmers, shopkeepers, factory managers, etc. Then things could be run in accordance with local needs and conditions, and would no doubt run much better. But this would be against the communist policy of centralisation; it is necessary for all decisions to tie in with the national plan so that the economy is organised efficiently and effectively.

But the rulers' decisions will be a reflection of their beliefs rather than their knowledge. If they like electric trains, the whole country will have electric trains. If they think that people should have 'sensible' shoes rather than frivolous, fashionable ones, the whole country will have sensible shoes. If they think that big factories are the epitome of efficiency, then everyone will work in a big factory. If they believe that history, agriculture, Marxism, or any other subject which they happen to approve of should feature strongly in education, then such subjects will be emphasised in every school in the country.

In fact, every aspect of life, both politically and economically, will be controlled by the individual or group at the apex of the state pyramid. And we have no reason to assume that they will relinquish such power, even if we believe that they are acting with the best of intentions. Good intentions do not always entail ideal behaviour; a person may continue 'doing their best' long after it is necessary, and perhaps do harm because of it. If they have taken power to guide their people through a difficult period, they must think that they are the ones most suited to the task. Therefore, everything that they do is in the population's best interests, whether the people agree with them or not. They are, after all, only trying to improve things, and if some cynical individuals impute selfish motives to their actions, well, its only human nature to resent great concentrations of power.

Even if the person in office does have benevolent attitudes, we still have to consider the next person to take over. For example, Tito was head of state of Yugoslavia, probably the most democratic socialist country in existence; but the next person to take office may be an unmitigated tyrant. Admittedly, there is the possibility of the next ruler being an improvement; China has become noticeably more liberal since the death of Mao. But the crucial factor remains that the quality of life in such a country is determined not by the structure of the system, but by pure luck.

But will there come a time when the country no longer needs some form of centralised control, and the state can wither away? For the foreseeable future the answer must be no. As long as governments think that they have the right to take over, or impose their will on, neighbouring countries, the armies and armed forces in general are necessary. And these must be controlled on a national level to ensure an effective strategy. Transport and communications should also be controlled nationally, and perhaps there should be centrally planned facilities to aid regions with economic disadvantages.

At the very minimum defence, transport, and communications must be a state prerogative. In addition there are the services that must be provided by local authorities—health, education, housing, water, etc. Accepting that all these facilities *must* be provided, then it becomes difficult to claim that the central state can ever be disposed of.

But it is not the entire state that withers away, only one aspect of it. Lenin says that *"under capitalism we have the state in the proper sense of the word, that is, a special machine for the suppression of one class by another . . ."*[1]

1. V.I. Lenin, op. cit.

During the transitional phase *"a special machine for suppression the 'state', is still necessary . . ."*[1] But when there is no private ownership, there can be no exploitation: *"The state withers away in so far as there are no longer any capitalists, any classes, and, consequently, no class can be suppressed."*[2] *"The government of persons is replaced by the administration of things and the direction of the processes of production."*[3]

So when the capitalists are no longer a threat, and classes have ceased to exist, the state as an instrument of oppression comes to an end. But the question of whether or not state power is still needed is one that is decided by those who control the state, and there is no way of ensuring that the dispersal of the machinery of oppression follows immediately after the end of its usefulness. The question reverts once again to whether or not the rulers will voluntarily relinquish their power. But to some people it is the power itself that is the most attractive aspect of the transitional state; great concentrations of power naturally draw to themselves people who seek authority and influence, and the majority of people in such positions will be those who wish to be, purely for the sake of the authority and prestige.

And as long as there are some services which must be supplied nationally, the people who wish to remain in office can still claim that the state is necessary. Perceptive and unselfish leaders would be willing to disperse the oppressive parts of the state, and devolve power to regional authorities, but then, whether or not the state is transitory depends on the character of the individuals in each particular situation. The only circumstance in which the controller, or group of controllers, would give up their office or a significant portion of their authority, would be if they were genuinely

1. Lenin, op. cit.
2. Lenin, op. cit.
3. F. Engels *Anti-Duhring*.

acting with the best of intentions, and the centralised co-ordination and instruments of suppression were no longer needed, *and* the rulers had the perception to realise that many decisions have to be taken at a local level. All three conditions have to apply, simultaneously, before the state will come to an end.

But when constructing a system of absolute power it is not enough to say that it will come to an end in some cases, that it will wither away—sometimes. When one is creating a dictatorship nothing less than cast-iron guarantees are acceptable; but there are no laws, no guarantees—only the whims of unpredictable personalities. And for the transition to communism to be so dependent on individual character is a total negation of the historic inevitability claimed by Marxists. For the theory to be valid it should not be a case of 'If the leader is honest and perceptive, then . . .' It should be possible to say that in all circumstances, regardless of individual personality, the transition will occur, automatically. But this is not what happens.

The dictatorship of the proletariat, which from a logical or practical point of view is not actually necessary, was not even justifiable at the time that Marx was writing. Its laws are not those of historic inevitability, but of personal whim. It could become a benevolent autocracy, or it could lead to a system as harsh as that of Nazi Germany. And it is not transitory; once it comes into existence it is permanent. Only the state officials themselves can dissolve it, but they are the ones with the most to lose from doing so.

The teachings of Marx lead us to a dead end. One that is unavoidable if Marxist policies are adhered to, but just as certainly, one that most people would want to avoid.

4

Erewhon Unvisited

The Communist Utopia

According to Marx, the dictatorship of the proletariat *"only constitutes the transition"* to the communist society; but everywhere it remains fixed in this 'transitional' form. No socialist state has yet converted to communism, and none of them shows any signs of being likely to do so.

But the most interesting facet of this paradox of Marxism is the shortage of literature on communism. There are of course, books on Marxist theories of value, dialectical materialism, and critiques of capitalism and imperialism; but virtually no books describing the actual structure and operation of the intended future communist state. In fact Lenin once complained that he could find nothing in the works of Marx which dealt with the practicalities of the future society, the economic structure, and the way it should be run. August Bebel's book is the only one that this writer has been able to find which does try to describe how communism would work in practice.

Although Engels does refer to the work of Robert Owen, *"the clear-cut quality of whose communism leaves nothing to be desired."*[1] He also refers to Owen's *Book of the New*

1. F. Engels   Anti-Duhring.

Moral World in which can be found   *"not only the most clear-cut communism possible, with equal obligation to labour and equal rights in the product . . . but also the most comprehensive building project of the future communist society . . ."*[1] including *"complete estimates of costs of founding them, yearly expenditure, and probable revenue. And in his definite plan of the future, the technical working out of details is managed with such practical knowledge (ground plan, front and side and bird's-eye views all included) that the Owen method of social reform once accepted, there is little to be said against the actual arrangement of details."*[2]

From this is could be concluded that Engels, and presumably Marx as well, were so whole-heartedly in agreement with Owen that there was nothing they could add, and nothing they would alter. They did not need to write about the practicalities of communism because Owen had already said everything that needed to be said. But it is unusual for Marx and Engels to be so completely in agreement with anybody; at one time or another, nearly every one of their colleagues came in for some stinging criticism—Lassalle, Kautsky, Liebknecht, and even Bebel. Their view of things was so rigid, and so comprehensive, that they were constitutionally incapable of agreeing with everyone all the time.

But they agreed with Owen. Except for certain minor reservations; Owen did not believe in a violent revolution, or in centralisation, or the abolition of money. And, more significantly, *"He introduced as transition measures to the complete communistic organization of society, on the one hand, co-operative societies for retail trade and production."*[3] If Owen's beliefs were correct, then the

1. Engels, op. cit.
2. Engels, op cit.
3. Engels, op. cit.

transition to communism could be achieved by businessmen such as Owen—and Engels, had he wished—forming profitable business communities like that of New Lanark, Scotland, and gradually converting them to co-operative ownership.

If this was valid then the entire theoretical apparatus of Marxism was scrap. Historic inevitability was meaningless, the transitional state was redundant, and even the ultimate phase of communism was transformed—into a co-operatively owned, non-centralised economy, owned directly by the workers themselves. A revolution, violent or otherwise, becomes unnecessary, and the centralised repression that was considered vital to keep the old capitalists in line ceases to be valid. And the iron laws of capitalist accumulation which were used to prove the inevitability of a revolution, become laws that lead to nothing, and prove nothing.

In normal circumstances Marx and Engels were scathingly critical of their opponents, indeed, Marx stated that it was important to utterly destroy the credibility of pseudo-socialists, as they channeled the workers' efforts into false and fruitless tasks. But in the *Manifesto* there is only the mild comment that Owen's work was premature in relation to the development of class antagonisms, while Engels had little to say against the actual details.

But whatever the reasons for their failing to criticise Owen, it is obvious that Owen's beliefs could not coincide with those of Marx and Engels. The method of change, the transitional period, and the final communist society were all things which they held unique views on. But the last, and most important phase, was the one that they spent the least effort in describing.

It is simply not possible to reconcile Owen's communism with that of Marx and Engels, but at least they could have followed his example, and using their laws of economic relationships, worked out details of how the future society should be structured. It would not even be necessary to go into the sort of detail that Owen did, with estimates of yearly expenditure and revenue, and architectural plans of the buildings. But at least they could have laid out the general principles.

This failure to examine communism is not only the greatest paradox of Marxism, but also its greatest weakness. Communism should be the central issue of both communist theory and of its followers' beliefs; it is supposed to be what all the various types of communist groups are aiming for; it is their goal, the reason they believe in communism. Well, obviously it isn't, because if it was there would be many more books describing the shape of the future society, and Bebel's name would be as well-known as those of Marx, Lenin, or Trotsky.

But Bebel's work is not outstandingly well-known, in fact, he is ignored to the point of total obscurity. And the actual structure of the proposed society is also regarded with the utmost indifference. The explanation for this must be that people are attracted to communism for irrational reasons; they are more concerned with social change than with social improvement. They are more interested in the drama of a revolution than in the society which the revolution is supposed to bring. They may be more interested in creating a dictatorship and 'coming to power' than in improving the welfare of the average worker. But undeniably, communism is not of any noticeable concern to the average communist.

This lack of interest must be the most damning indictment of all that could be levelled against modern communists, and must surely cast grave doubts on the integrity of their motives. If they are not interested in the ultimate society, then what are they interested in? If they are not aiming for that particular goal, then what are they aiming for? The answer will vary for each individual, but would range from a simple fascination with the drama of great events, to, at the other end of the scale, egotism and megalomania.

Marx himself must take some of the blame for this unbalanced attitude on the part of his adherents. His major works were just criticisms of the economic system of his time, and although his attacks were fully justified, by themselves they are not enough. He should not have stopped at the transitional phase, but should have gone on to analyse in detail the structure and practicalities of the future society. Had he done so, he might have discovered some of many contradictions in the theory, and perhaps he could have re-worked it into a more practical and beneficial system. But in failing to do this he also failed to attract people who would have been sympathetic to his underlying principles, but were put off by the methods proposed.

Instead Marx seems to have attracted supporters with a remarkable talent for ignoring the basic moral issues, and transferring the emphasis to the transitional dictatorship. Again, this is Marx's fault. In addition to the stress that Marx placed of the lower phase, there is also his attitude to the preaching of morality. Isiah Berlin says that Marx was intensely suspicious of the high-flown claims and language of some moralists, regarding it as no more than a front for some hidden dishonesty. Because of this, he deliberately avoided making any strident moral claims or assertions, relying instead on the morality inherent in his criticisms.

But this was merely an academic failing; a much more serious responsibility must fall on the shoulders of modern Marxists. They have taken Marx's understatement of the moral issues, and his lack of practical detail on communism, and extended it to its illogical conclusion—by completely ignoring the moral issues, *and* the structure of communism. The writings of August Bebel have been almost totally ignored, and no contemporary Marxist has attempted to develop a more modern view of the intended society. A revision of Bebel's work is long overdue, because much has happened to make his book out of date regarding possible technology, the use of that technology, and indeed, the ιype of society that should be aimed for.

But as there is no modern analysis of communism, I shall make use of Bebel's book, *Society of the Future*, plus the few hints that are available in Marx's own work.

So, assuming that the lower phase has somehow passed on—despite the extreme improbability of this—or that it has been excluded from the course of development, we arrive at the ultimate communist society. With all factories, farms, and so on communally owned, classes would cease to exist; there would no longer be any property distinctions as everyone owns the means of production. There would be no exploitation, as the wealth produced would be distributed equally; nor could there be exploitation , as no-one owned the factories to any greater degree than anyone else. With the end of classes and of exploitation, the repressive mechanisms of the state are abolished, and the higher phase of communism is attained.

So what is it? For a start, it is a totally centralised system. Marx was opposed to federalism, regarding it as a dubious idea derived from bourgeois anarchism. All ownership, and all administration will be totally centralised. Naturally, decision-making will be as well, but will *all* decisions be taken centrally? The administrative system would then be deciding on the size, design, structural content, and fitting of all new houses, shops, factories, offices, hospitals, schools, and warehouses. It would have to control the range of products, the design, the materials and machinery used in every manufacturing process in the country. Its control would also extend to agriculture of course, but this would mean that all farming would be run from the nation's capital city; and Marx had intended to reduce the antithesis between town and country.

Bebel suggested that the gradual increase in the size of big cities would be reversed, that *"the population of the big cities will migrate to the country, form new communities there, adapted to the changed conditions, and will combine industrial with agricultural activity."*[1] But he goes on to say that *"Decentralisation will also abolish the existing antithesis between the rural and the urban population."*[2]

So on the one hand we have the straight Marxist line, with total centralisation of control, including farms administered from the city. On the other hand is Bebel's view, which eliminates the antithesis, but still fails to follow the Marxist line on centralisation. But Marx's own work contradicts itself on exactly this point; it is not possible to adhere to his principles on both points. According to the Manifesto, *"The bourgeoisie has subjected the country to the rule of the towns."*[3] Under communism, things will be different; the proletariat will control the subjection.

The image suggested by these various descriptions is of a society with a great deal of farming activity, many small and medium sized towns, and one huge administrative capital city. A slightly unbalanced arrangement, but apart from that, quite reasonable.

The next problem is what sort of factories, machinery, and production processes will be used in industry. Marx objected to capitalist industry making the workman an appendage of the machine, his skills rendered worthless, his job turned into monotonous repetition. To eliminate this, under communism there would be a return to more labour intensive, skilled forms of production; the worker would become a creative craftsman instead of a mere attendant. He

1. August Bebel   *Society of the Future.*
2. Bebel, op. cit.
3. Marx and Engels   *The Manifesto of the Communist Party.*

would panel-beat car bodies, rather than just place the sheet steel in a stamping press; he could actually make furniture instead of endlessly cutting out one part; and bakers would make real bread, and get away from the rolling production lines of cooked, processed flour.

All this would be fine except for two points. First, the way in which each job was re-designed would be controlled by the central administration. Somebody at head office would decide which over-capitalised machinery would be removed, which production processes would be eliminated, and which tools and materials are to be introduced in their place. The workers will be free of drudgery, and able to exercise their creativity, but only within the exact limits set by the controllers. Without the freedom to work as one wants, there cannot be any real creativity, but what constraints are placed on working methods should be decided by people who understand the work. To have the processes determined by distant bureaucrats is a negation of the whole purpose of the change.

The second problem is that Marx objected to the burden of toil imposed by work, and to the long hours. *"With the present development of the productive forces, coupled with the abolition . . . of the waste of products and means of production, resulting from the capitalist mode of production, will suffice, with everybody doing his share of work, to reduce the time required for labour to a point which, measured by our present conceptions, will be small indeed."*[1]

Bebel takes the argument a stage further, suggesting that production be concentrated in large factories, citing as evidence a survey which showed that big factories, although few in number, *"produced almost two and a half times as much as all the other establishments taken together. But the big establishments could also be rationalised considerably,*

1. F. Engels *Anti-Duhring.*

so that if the whole of production were to be organised in accordance with the most advanced technology, a much larger quantity of work could be done."[1]

Bebel then quotes a survey of estimated labour needs in Austria, which found that each worker "*would have to work only 36.9 days, about 6 weeks, to produce the means of subsistence for 22 million people. If we take 300 working days instead of 37, then, with the new organisation of labour, and estimating the duration of the present working day as eleven hours, it would require only 1⅛ hours to satisfy the most essential requirements.*"[2]

If the working day at that time was eleven hours, then neither Engels nor Bebel would have been much impressed with the current 8 hour day; but less than two hours is another matter. But it also seems unlikely, given the state of last century's technology; yet this does not invalidate the argument, as with modern methods—micro-chips, robots, and computerised automation—such working hours do seem possible. It would not be practical to mechanise to such a degree in a capitalist country, as the removal of most of the workforce—the practical result of low staffing needs—would mean massive levels of unemployment; and very few people with the money to buy things.

But it is quite in line with communist principles to continue paying wages to the whole workforce, regardless of the fact that the majority of them are unemployed. Nonetheless, it is important to consider the conditions under which they will work. It is probable that they will work in big factories—perhaps the biggest possible. There may be some modern Marxists who have noted and learned from the lessons of the twenties, when factories were built on the very principle that Bebel—and at the end of that era, Stalin virtually apologised for the mistakes and excesses of 'giantism'.

1. August Bebel, op. cit.
2. Bebel, op. cit.

But it is a lesson that is not easily learnt. Big factories and big business continue to enchant left-wing politicians, even though there is no rational reason for it; the absence of rationality has never stopped politicians yet. It was the Labour government of 1964 – 1970 that created British Leyland, British Steel, and British Airways; had these mergers been successful, it would have been glorious proof of the correctness of Labour's vision; as failures, they prove nothing. Big business is also not falsifiable.

Corporation executives also seem fascinated by the idea of great size; although it is doubtful that a Freudian psychologist would phrase it in those terms. Fiat have created in Turin a car assembly point that is one of the largest in the world, working on the principle that big is more efficient; perhaps it is—in purely technical terms. Unfortunately, Fiat forgot to take the human factor into account; the same mistake that Marx made. The sheer size of the factory gives the workers a feeling of insignificance and non-involvement; the feeling of alienation which Marx regarded as one of the faults of capitalism.

Big factories and automation may eliminate the toil and long hours that Marx disliked, but apart from causing alienation, it will also turn the worker back into an append-age of the machinery. *"Nay, more, in proportion as the use of machinery and division of labour increases, in the same proportion the burden of toil also increases . . ."*[1] But to bring back *"all individual character, and, consequently, all charm for the workman . . ."*[2] and to make the work genuinely creative, requires less mechanisation.

It is probable that a compromise system could be developed, with medium levels of technology, and thus offer sufficient creativity to satisfy the worker, yet remain efficient enough

1. Marx and Engels, op. cit.
2. Marx and Engels, op. cit.

to give him reasonable hours. But if we are considering this compromise purely from the worker's point of view—which is the only one that Marx thought about—then it is obvious that the only person qualified to judge the alternatives is the worker himself. He must weigh up the gains in job satisfaction against the losses of longer working hours; no distant bureaucrat can ever be qualified to make this decision for him.

There is also the danger that if the worker seeks too much creativity, the product will become so expensive that few can afford it. Or, as the final phase will be a non-monetary economy, the goods will be so scarce that few will be able to find them. The worker's requirements must be balanced against those of the population in general, and to allow the workers total control would be almost as bad as giving it to the bureaucrats. Another compromise must be arranged by the factory manager, weighing the workers' needs against those of the customers.

But how will customers acquire goods, and what is there to limit their consumption if there are no monetary restrictions placed on them? In the early stages, the worker *"receives a certificate from society that he has furnished such and such an amount of labour . . . and with this certificate he draws from the social stock of means of consumption as much as the same amounts of labour costs. The same amount of labour which he has given to society in one form he receives back in another."*[1]

Thus, the workers is not paid in money; it is merely proof of the labour he has performed, and so is proof of his entitlement to goods. But certificates are not given equally—*"one man is superior to another physically or mentally and so supplies more labour in the same time, or can work for a longer time; and labour, to serve as a measure, must be defined by its duration or intensity, otherwise it ceases to be*

1. Karl Marx   *Critique of the Gotha Programme.*

a standard of measurement. This equal right is an unequal right for unequal labour."[1]

"*Further, one worker is married, another is not; one has more children than another, and so on and so forth. Thus, with an equal performance of labour, and hence an equal share in the social consumption fund, one will in fact receive more than another . . .*"[2]

So in the transitional phase there will be a series of compensatory arrangements so that each worker is paid according to the amount and quality of his work, and according to his family needs. But in the higher phase, this system of allocation is done away with. Marx says that "*after the enslaving subordination of the individual to the division of labour, and with it also the antithesis between mental and physical labour, has vanished . . . then can the narrow horizon of bourgeois right be crossed in its entirety and society inscribe on its banners: From each according to his ability, to each according to his needs!*"[3]

Allocation and unequal rights will have been eliminated, and in their place, every worker will be expected to work as well and as hard as he can, while in return he will be allowed to take exactly what he needs. At least this does not openly contradict some other aspect of Marxism, but it does seem somewhat impractical. There are no longer any financial inducements to make anyone work harder, or even work at all; what he does has no effect on his standard of living; he can work as little as he wants, and help himself to as much as he wants. Nor is there any point in his working harder now in order to have more leisure in the future; he can work as little as he wants now, and then do the same in the future.

Such a system might be practical in small communities,

1. Marx, op. cit.
2. Marx, op. cit.
3. Marx, op. cit.

such as those set up by Owen, but on a national level it would be much harder to control. Any work evasion by one person throws the burden of labour onto other workers, which in a small community means friends and neighbours. The lazy person knows exactly who is taking the burden, and they in turn know who is creating it. When the extra work is effectively shared out amongst the entire workforce, it is much easier for someone to claim that no-one will notice any difference. A national economy is too large and impersonal to allow such luxuries as the freedom not to work, or the right to take as many consumer goods as one wants.

Marx claimed that with the transition to communism would come a total transformation of human nature, and perhaps he believed that people would act and think in a way completely different from the way they do now. There is no doubt that people's behaviour and attitudes vary according to circumstance, but for Marx to claim that a complete transformation would occur is less than rational. After all, two of the major faults of Marxism are the inability to describe the structure of the future system, and an inability to take human factors into account. These comprise a very poor basis from which to predict a transformation of human attitudes created by the new system.

Marx said that the structure of the economic system moulds men's beliefs and their way of thinking; but if he couldn't describe the structure, then he couldn't predict the patterns of thought that would exist. Therefore, he could not predict that a transformation would take place. And if this is true, then the practicality of his free, self-service economy is in doubt—to put it mildly. So Marx's failure to put down the details of his intended system is, in itself, a major weakness in his theory, but by his own logic it ceases to be possible to say what social attitudes will be—which invalidates Marx's ideas on payment for labour, and distribution of goods.

"Not indulging in utopias, Marx expected the experience of the mass movement to provide the answer to the question as to what specific forms this organization of the proletariat as the ruling class will assume . . ."[1]   Lenin was referring here to the transitional phase, but perhaps Marx believed that the same was true of the higher phase, and that may be why he failed to describe it in detail. But the above objection still holds true; if he did not know the structure, then he could not know the patterns of thought. If the actual structure could only be clarified by the process of social change, then attitudes can only be assessed after the process had finished.

Nor is it rational to regard all attempts to describe the ideal society as *"indulging in utopias"*.   If there is logical or empirical evidence for the practicality and superiority of such a society, then it is not utopianism, but creating an outline for social improvement. And if Marx's laws and relationships were scientifically valid, then he should have been able to describe his ideal system in reasonable detail. If the economic environment affects society, then it should have been possible for him to decide what sort of society he was aiming for, and working backwards, calculate what type of economy would be needed to create the necessary conditions.

But the few items that have been analysed so far are the only ones that Marx stated with any degree of precision; there are still a large number of questions unanswered. For example, how is ownership to be defined or described, where is it formally located, what written guarantees of ownership should exist? Lenin refers to a time when   *"equality is achieved for all members of society* in relation to ownership of the means of production."*[2]   (emphasis in original). But how will this be achieved? Should ownership be formalised

---

1. V.I. Lenin   *The State and Revolution.*
2. Lenin, op. cit.

by the workers having shares in the factory they work for? Should the local council be the official owner, or should everything be owned by the state?

Marx was fully aware of the existence of joint stock companies, and mentioned them quite a few times in *Capital*. He was therefore aware of the fact that control of the factors of production could be attained without having ownership; and that the possession of ownership did not necessarily give control. In view of Marx's apparent intentions, one would have thought that formal, paper ownership was not what he had in mind. But he should have been able to see the possibility of types of ownership developing in which the workers had full, legal ownership, but no actual control. And presumably it was worker control that was Marx's real concern in proposing worker ownership.

In the absence of any statement to the contrary, it could only be assumed that Marx intended the centralised ownership of the transitional phase to continue into the final phase; which is what most people have assumed. But this form does not give the equality of ownership that Lenin referred to, and that Marx would presumably have agreed with. In failing to specify how the means of production should be owned in the communist phase, Marx was implicitly accepting a form of ownership which could never give equal control, and could give the workers no control whatsoever.

Control and ownership are two of the central themes of Marxism, even though they are not always stated explicitly. The worker sells his labour for a pittance because he has to, he has no other way of making a living—he owns no means of production. The capitalist owns—or manages on the shareholders' behalf—the factory where the worker is employed; whether he owns or manages, he controls, so he is the one who fixes wage levels. The worker has no power to control his way of life because he neither owns nor controls the productive forces; the capitalist has power because he owns; and if he does not own, he controls.

By implication, Marx replaces this with a system in which everyone owns—on paper—so everyone is a shareholder in the new economy. But there is still a small and separate group that controls, that decides what will be made, in what quantities, how it will be distributed, and how much the workers will be paid.

By failing to state where control and ownership would be located, and how they would be formalised, Marx was by his own standards failing to define the economic relations that would exist. The choices that he could have specified ranged from the common ownership proposed by Robert Owen, to centrally co-ordinated joint stock companies managed locally, to the type that has become automatically associated with Marxism—the centrally owned and controlled economy. But in failing to select a suitable possibility, Marx was unable to predict the economic relations that would exist, the social relations that result from them, and the patterns of thought that develop with a given type of social relations.

The lack of any explicitly stated ownership structure means that Marx—and all subsequent Marxists—are unable to make any valid statements at all concerning the form of society they propose. To return to Kant's dictum, any statement can be made with just as much validity as any other; all such opinions would be equally lacking in logic or evidence, so all would be equally meaningless. And if there is no way of knowing anything about the social or economic structure of communism, there is little of value that can be said for the ideology of communism.

To take another case, how would the economy—and society—be administered? By central control, by co-ordination, or by consensus? Lenin claims that *"Engels did not at all understand democratic centralism in the bureaucratic sense in which this term is used by bourgeois and petty bourgeois ideologists . . . His idea of centralism did not in the least preclude such broad local self-government as would combine the voluntary defence of the unity of the state by the 'communes' and provinces with the complete abolition of all bureaucratic practices and all 'ordering' from above."*[1]

Perhaps Engels' ideas did not preclude the possibility of local government, but on the other hand, that does not mean that he actively endorsed it. And what is democratic centralism—which Lenin definitely supported—if there is no ordering from above? If it is centralism with no centralisation, then it is a contradiction. Lenin does not clarify what he means, so as it stands, his statement is virtually meaningless.

"It is extremely important to note that Engels, armed with facts, disproves by a most precise example the prejudice which is very widespread . . . that a federal republic necessarily means a greater amount of freedom than a centralized republic. This is wrong . . . the greatest *amount of local, provincial and other freedom known in history was accorded by a* centralized *and not by a federal republic."*[2] (emphasis in original).

So both Engels and Lenin may have believed in local government, with no ordering from above. Also, Marx, Engels, and Lenin subscribed to the ideas of democratic centralism, with a centralised state. Which tells us absolutely nothing about the system they are actually proposing. But in view of the frequency of references to centralism and centralisation, one can assume that this was the type of structure they had in mind. But if all one can do is assume,

1. V.I. Lenin, op. cit.
2. Lenin, op. cit.

then the theory has not been constructed with very great precision.

So how will things be run, and on what principles? Who will it be run by, how will they be chosen, how will they be controlled, what powers will they have, how will they balance the needs of workers and consumers? And to what degree will there be an electoral democracy?

What counterbalances would there be to protect the rights of the people, and what would the constitution be? Lenin objected to people who imagined that a new society, with totally new goals and ideals, could be expected to start life complete with a written constitution, comprehensive laws, and all the other formal paraphernalia of legislation. But Marx could have used the constitution of the 1871 Paris Commune as a basis, or the American Constitution, and modified either one according to his own opinions.

Perhaps a complete constitution is not actually necessary, but in view of the uncertainty regarding the structure of the system, and its goals and intentions, it would have been a good idea to include a brief description of the main popular rights. For example, whether or not people would have the right to vote, have impartial justice, and freedom of speech. Possibly Marx took these basic rights for granted, and felt they were not worth specifying, but considering the frequent condemnations of democracy it would be important to define what sort of system would take its place. A basic definition is essential, but even the briefest description would have been sufficient. For example, Marx could merely have mentioned that he thought the system should be an electoral democracy, or have consensus based on local meetings, or have referenda on major issues. But instead we have no information at all.

Who creates and phrases new legislation? Who decides the general issues on which laws are to be based, and who controls or selects the people who make the laws? And who controls the judiciary? In describing the Paris Commune, Marx writes that *"magistrates and judges were to be elective, responsible, and revocable."*[1] But this is merely describing another system; it is by no means certain that Marx intended the same rules to apply to communism.

And who takes economic decisions, such as where to concentrate investment, or what production methods to use? How do they balance the conflicting needs of workers and consumers, how do they decide what goods are worth making, and what would be done for people who need goods and services other than the normal consumer products? For instance, how would they treat people with minority interests and hobbies, or the disabled or chronically sick; who would decide whether or not to manufacture kidney dialysis machines?

In an electoral democracy, the majority vote for one particular party to look after their intersts, and quite often the needs of minority groups are ignored. In a centralised economy the same indifference to the wishes of some minorities must also occur. As soon as one takes the stance that the central administration will follow policies aimed at maximising general welfare, one is unavoidably involved in a policy of indifference to minorities.

It is in the nature of centralised administration to deal in broad outlines, national planning, the overall pattern; after all, if policies are to be planned and implemented on a local basis, there is no point in centralising. It is a system that is not designed to, nor can it cope with, the individual quirks of each and every person that makes up the population. If it asks everyone what he or she wants to do, and then tells them to do it, firstly, it is creating a massive quantity of work for itself, and second, the orders given are redundant and meaningless. The administration would be better off

1. Karl Marx   *The Civil War in France*, cited in Lenin, op. cit.

dissolving itself, and leaving people to choose and act for themselves. If it asks, but ignores the answers, then it will be ignoring individual welfare, and damaging personal happiness. If it does not ask at all, then the harm to personal welfare will be even greater; but average welfare may be served.

Apart from the problem of identifying minority needs, there is also the fact that any of the economy's resources devoted to mass-consumption goods cannot be used for minority interest goods. There is only so much labour, or capital, or machinery available; and if it is being used to produce radio sets for the masses, it cannot be used to make heart pace-makers. There is an unavoidable conflict of interests, and centralisation of decisions is the least effective way of reconciling this conflict.

The fact is that centralisation is bad, whether it is capitalist or communist. The difference is that in a communist society the state has even greater powers than normal, while the population has less reciprocal control over the state.

Most western democracies are far from perfect. The affluent majority totally ignore the needs of the poor; politicians follow a strange path comprised of dogma, vote-catching, and preserving the status quo; big business uses its considerable lobbying power to ensure that no laws which are harmful to industry can ever be introduced; and the rich continue to grow richer. But all this is no reason to say that we should have communism instead. If the existing system is imperfect, we should either modify it to make it better, or seek a superior alternative. And communism has yet to prove itself superior to capitalism. Yet even if it did, it would not be enough; what it has to do is prove itself to be totally superior, the best possible system that could exist.

It may be superior to the transitional phase, where the state as an instrument of oppression has withered away, but this superiority is only potential, depending on the exact structure of the system. There is still the lack of any consistent attitude to moral issues, the contradiction between abolishing the urban/rural antithesis and the centralised administration, and the conflicting requirements of the workforce, seeking both creativity and reasonable hours.

There is the early Marxist belief in big factories, that has been carried on to modern times by some left-wing politicians, but this conflicts with the desire to give the worker humane and human working conditions, and an atmosphere that does not alienate and oppress. And the free distribution of goods is only possible if there is a transformation of human nature; but without knowing what the structure of society will be, it is impossible to say how human nature will be changed by it.

Communism—the higher phase—has almost as many contradictions in it as the dictatorship of the proletariat. And the reason for this is perhaps the biggest contradiction of all; communists aren't interested in communism. Engels describes a revolution as being *"the most authoritarian thing there is."* He regards the methods of revolution, the weapons, and the terror that is inspired, as all being part of the same necessary, authoritarian process. Perhaps what really attracts people to Marxism is revolution and the resultant dictatorship, and if this is true, then Marxism is not a left-wing ideology at all. Marxism, especially as it is conceived and practiced by some modern Marxists, is actually a very right-wing, authoritarian ideology.

It is probably not possible to create a totally consistent system, operating within the definitions that Marx and Engels used, but if they believed that it was possible, then they should have given it whatever precision and detail they could. By criticising the system and yet failing to offer a detailed alternative, Marx was in effect saying, observe the faults in your system—here, here, and here; I propose a new system which I shall describe as follows—it must be better. Which, to put it mildly, is not a very useful basis for creating social change.

But despite all the objections, Marxism may still be practical. That is, it may be possible to run a country along the general lines described by Marx, adhering to the principles if not to the details. But this could only be done if a centralised economy can be run effectively; so the next chapter will examine the workings of such an economy.

5

Orders from Above

The Command Economy

After the state as a means of oppression has withered away, *"the government of persons is replaced by the administration of things, and by the conduct of processes of production"*.[1] Marx had clearly specified that the economy would be centralised, and in the *Gotha Programme* he described a system of allocation of goods during the transitional phase, with totally free availability in the 'higher' phase.

From this Marxists developed the idea of the command economy, a planned centralised, carefully ordered, non-monetary economy. Allocation of raw materials, investment, and consumer goods are all planned, and everything is arranged in the most logical, rational, and therefore most efficient way. Factories, mills, and warehouses would all be located for the maximum efficiency, with no double journeys, no unnecessary transport or production, and no wastage.

At first glance it seems to be an extremely logical system. The state decides the probable demand for every type of consumer goods, and from that, calculates the quantity and type of every raw material, fuel source, machine, and

1. F. Engels *Anti-Duhring*.

transport system needed to make and supply the goods.

For example, supposing the demand for chairs is predicted to be one million units next year. Of these, half will be made of wood, and the remainder will be steel and plastic. The state will then ensure that the factories are supplied with the necessary quantities of wood, steel, and plastic to make the required chairs. In turn, lumber mills must have the saws, saw blades, electricity, and wood preservative needed to cut and treat the required quantity of wood; steel mills must have the correct amount of iron ore, coke, and carbon, plus blast furnace and rolling capacity; and plastic manufacturers must have the right amount of crude oil, dyestuffs, and all the conversion and polymerisation equipment necessary.

The state, as overseer of the manufacturing process, ensures that everyone in the chain of manufacture has all the materials and equipment needed to make the goods that people want. It can also ensure that resources go towards things that people genuinely need, and are not squandered on trivial luxuries. We should not have the sort of society in which the wealthy can buy gold-plated cocktail stirrers, while the poor cannot even afford to buy food. The communist state would give priority to essential supplies, and luxury goods would only be made if there was a surplus of resources.

Thus, the centralised economy can not only ensure efficiency, it also allocates resources with more justice than capitalism does—so the argument goes. But if one studies how the command economy works in practice, a number of faults become apparent. How does the state know what people want, or need; can it distinguish between valid and frivolous requirements; and even assuming the best possible motives on the part of administrators, how can we be sure that people will actually get what they want? Is the command economy really efficient, or is it by its very nature taking on too much to be efficient? And is it really the great advance that communists claim, replacing selfishness—the profit motive—with general welfare as the driving force in the economy?

It resolves down to two basic questions: one, is the system morally defensible—a subjective question, devoid of scientific content, and concerned purely with the welfare of human beings. Two, is it practical, is it really as efficient as it is claimed to be?

To justify the introduction of a command economy, it must not only be proved that it is workable, it must be possible to prove that it is as efficient as the market economy, or more so. Alternatively, it should be proved that any loss of efficiency is made up for by the improvement in welfare.

But the command economy had a considerable disadvantage; to follow Marx's creed it must be a non-monetary economy. Goods do not have a price, they are allocated according to need. The logical consequence of this policy, extended throughout the economy, is that no stage in the production process has any money value or cost attached to it; there are no prices, no profits, no rents, wages, or interest rates; no market economy.

The conventional market system contains built-in information mechanisms that are fully automatic—no extra staff are needed to collect, collate, or transmit information on the success of the organisation to its policy makers. In the free market, sales volumes indicate the level of consumer satisfaction; the customer is free to buy whatever he wants, from whoever he wishes to deal with, so if he buys from one company rather than another, it is because that company's products please him more. The firm is competing with other companies that are all busily trying to outsell it, so if a firm makes a profit, it is efficient; if it makes a larger profit than its competitors, then it is more efficient.

Sometimes in western societies sales and profits indicate

other things—socially negative things. They indicate the power of the corporation to dominate the market; which really means that in a monopoly economy, there is no free market. But the faults in the existing economies do not prove the validity or necessity of the Marxist alternative; merely that some form of change is needed.

To prove the validity of the Marxist economy it must be possible to show that the technical efficiencies of the command economy are greater than the cost of the managerial complexities of the bureaucratic transfer of information. But without money, without some form of accounting system, it is not easy to say which part works well, or which works badly. We can only look at the results. The shops are closed for as many as ten working days out of a hundred, and when they are open, there are shortages inside, and long queues outside. And no-one seems to know why.

   For any economy, money has the great advantage of being an indicator; it shows that given a limited range of products to buy, and having a limited amount of money to spend on them, people will choose certain products, and leave others. They have to make a choice; and the goods that are bought are the ones that are at the top of each individual's list of personal preferences. Therefore, the goods that sell are the ones that are the most wanted of all the goods that could be produced. The price that goods sell at is an indicator of their cost of production—in labour, raw materials, machinery, fuel, etc. It also represents the effort that has been expended on the goods, an effort that can no longer be expended on any other product—it shows the opportunity costs, the possibilities that have been forgone.

Just as a consumer may forgo owning a colour television so that he can eat at good restaurants three times a week, similarly, every time society or the planners decide on one course of action, they are eliminating all the other possibilities. The consumer only has a limited amount of money, and society only has a certain amount of manpower, capital, and raw material. Building a rail link from one town to another means postponing the construction of a new shoe factory; financing a state opera house means less bread next year.

In capitalist countries money is moved from one sector to another via taxes, grants, and subsidies. The politicans decide what the people should have that they are not willing or able to pay for themselves—schools, hospitals, art galleries, motorways, and so on—then the government organises the transfer of money from one sector to another. Some things are done, others are left. The decisions are not always rational, but they can always be done on the basis of cost; it is known how much the state raises in tax in a year, equally, they know how much it costs to build a mile of motorway or 10,000 houses. So they know what the nation can afford.

Without knowledge of the costs involved, and the opportunities forgone, there can be no rational decision making whatsoever. Society may be investing more effort than it can spare, or it may be ignoring important policies in the belief that the resources are not available. There is no way of knowing how effective its policies are.

Nor is there any way of comparing normal economic processes; is a rail link more efficient than a motorway, is an automated factory more appropriate than an assembly line, is pre-fabricated construction better than conventional brick building? Each one uses up various amounts of labour, materials, capital, fuel, etc., but if all of these are free, then how can one say what the cost it?

And the comparative decisions just listed are the easy ones. When we get to the fine details of production, then things really get tricky. How does one compare lathe machining with spark erosion, electro-plating with vacuum plating, or brazing with arc welding? The choice becomes impossible.

And the problems would become even greater at the retail level, with goods being made freely available to consumers, as and when they wanted them. In practice it simply could not work, because if people can take whatever they want, their wants will tend to increase. When people have to pay for things, they are forced to take some care in deciding exactly which things to buy. The supply of money is limited, therefore the range of goods which can be purchased is also limited; so a choice must be made as regards the products to be bought. If all goods are free then the need for selection disappears, less thought will be applied to choosing goods, and more goods will be taken.

So the planners must make a choice—between a system of rationing to ensure that people do not take too many of the goods available, and a mass production economy, capable of turning out everything that anyone could want, without limit. To produce lots of everything, with an excess of supply over demand to allow for the highest possible level of demand for each style and colour of goods, must surely be the height of inefficiency. A system of rationing on the other hand, involves a fixed maximum output for each product, with a total rations level equal to the volume of output. But ration cards should be transferable, so that anyone who doesn't want their quota of a given product can give it to, or exchange it with, another consumer's card for a different product.

Considering the similarity between convertible cards and money, in view of the need for some carefully thought out order of priorities, and allowing for the effectiveness of money as a means of exchange, one can reasonably assume that any intelligently planned economy would have money as its basis of exchange. It may have materialist connotations, but one does not remove materialism by disposing of money; materialism is an attitude affecting human beings, not an inherent part of the printing process as it affects paper.

Most communist nations are aware of the value of money—as a means of exchange—and have not abolished it from their economies. Nor have they entirely abandoned the market economy, or even the concept of profits. Marx regarded profits as crystallised surplus value, and thus were both proof of, and the measure of, the degree of exploitation. According to Wilczynski, profit under socialism has no similarity except name with profit under capitalism.

Socialist profit is not an end in itself, but a way of measuring efficiency; but it is not necessarily a way of measuring efficiency, because prices are fixed by the state. Wilczynski claims each one of these contradictory items to be proof of the dissimilarity of socialist and capitalist profit; but they cannot both be true. Equally, he claims that profit cannot be raised by limiting output; but output *is* limited, and prices are fixed by the planners, therefore, high profits can be directly attributed to restricted output. Wilczynski's most important claim is that levels of profit do not control the allocation of domestic and foreign investment; but this does not create a distinction between the profit of socialist organisations and capitalist ones; it merely highlights the different political decisions made by the state. Apart from which, 'foreign investment', in the context of Russian policy-making, is a phrase that can cover a multitude of things.

To some degree the state does rely on price differentials and consumer demand in allocating production facilities, and there is a form of market economy. But this is in complete opposition to the type of structure that Marx had described, and so constitutes a rejection of original Marxist policy. Nor is it internally consistent; it creates a peculiar hybrid, with notional transfer prices between companies, and artificial prices at retail level. To make things even more complicated, retail prices are often topped up with a turnover tax which can be as high as 80% of the base price. Thus, the consumer is not paying the notional price of production, nor is it a market determined price. It is a price that balances normal demand with abnormally low supply, and is equivalent to the excessive prices that monopolies can charge when they restrict output. The fact that the tax goes to the state instead of the corporation (which is owned by the state) is a mere technicality.

According to Volkonskii,[1] there is no reason to regard planning and the market economy as contradictory. But the market is an information mechanism that requires free decision making at retail level, plus the ability and the willingness to adapt to consumer needs at production level. Planning involves centralised decision making, and the willingness of producers to follow orders from above. Thus, the two systems are totally in conflict.

Nor can this dubious hybrid be said to serve people—in any sense of the word. Because production is controlled by the planners instead of by the consumers' purchases, there will be less choice in what is available. Planning an economy is a difficult task, and there is no point in adding to the problems by creating new varieties of product. So each category of product will have a restricted range of colour, style, size, quality, and so on. There may even be no variety whatsoever, with goods available only in one basic form. And some types of product may simply not be available.

But despite its failure or unwillingness to provide the means for a full and varied life, the state can still persuade its citizens that it is doing its best—or that it is doing the best that is socially necessary. The state, using the mass media which it alone controls, can inform the people of its

1. cited by J. Wilczynski *The Economics of Socialism*, Allen and Unwin.

problems, and attach any credible explanation that it likes. No contrary facts or opinions can ever see the light of day.

But disregarding the material uniformity of life, is the command economy efficient? The answer to this depends on two things—the effectiveness of the planning system, and the effectiveness of those who administer the plan. If the plan is not comprehensive and accurate, it cannot work; and if those who carry out the plan are not capable or interested in fulfilling it, then it will not work.

The planning and control of an entire economy is a massively complex task. Each and every factory must produce exactly what is required of it in terms of type, quality, and quantity, for the consumer, or for whoever is involved in the next stage of production. This does not just mean putting people in the factories, and telling them to get on with it; they must be told in precise terms, and with accurate specifications, exactly what is required. A precise quantity and grade of each type of raw material must be produced; the right types of machinery and components must be made for each firm. And the needs of every single factory must be related to the output of every factory that it depends on.

The scale of the task may be gauged when one considers that in Russia there are 42,000 industrial units and 19,000 construction sites whose output is planned. There are two million items on the standard classification of industrial products manufactured in the Soviet Union. As regards raw materials, American scrap metal dealers distinguish 27 grades of aluminium, and 105 grades of iron and steel; but this is probably an underestimate of the actual variety of grades manufactured. It is not practical to use the same type of steel to make drill bits, surgical scalpels, electromagnets, and car body panels; and if one considers the thousands of different types and uses of steel, from shipbuilding to watches to saw blades, 105 types of iron and steel can only be the broadest categories.

The variety and number of producers, products, and raw materials is what creates the complexity of economic planning. The planners must relate total output of iron ore—and other raw materials—to every single use of iron and steel (or whatever) in the country; they must take account of every lathe, magnet, light switch, lorry, and filing cabinet that they will produce. They must supply the needs of every farm, factory, office, school, warehouse, building site, and retail outlet, and ensure that each one has whatever raw materials, semi-manufactures, components, finished products, and ancillary supplied that are needed.

The complexity of the task is so enormous in fact, that it cannot be done. In Russia only 40,000 products are actually covered by the central plan. But even for these few—40,000 items out of two million, just 2% of the economy—it is necessary to divide the plan amongst a number of ministries, commissions, and technical study groups. The primary policy decisions, what will actually be produced, are made by Gosplan, the State Planning Commission. The supplies needed are computed and allocated by Gosnab, the State Committee on Material-Technical Supply. Others involved include TSEMI, the Central Economic Mathematical Institute; TSU, the Central Statistical Administration; the Institute of Economics; and the Institute of Management Problems.

It is a massive bureacracy of experts and administrators, whose main function is to perform the information transmitting that is carried out automatically by the free market. The cost to the Soviety tax-payer is unknown, and if the system functioned reasonably well it might be worth asking if it was cost-effective. As it is, the only question worth asking is, why does it not operate efficiently?

As soon as Gosplan, with the assistance of TSEMI and TSU, has completed a necessary and reasonable plan, it

notifies the various ministries responsible for each category
of product, which then notify the sub-ministries, who
contact the regional ministries, and so on down to the
individual enterprises. Each enterprise has a certain
expected degree of efficiency, and has been allocated a
planned output, and a specific quantity of material inputs
with which to make the output goods. The manager of the
enterprise then states what he expects to be able to achieve,
and puts in a request for the materials and other inputs that
he expects to need.

The regional ministries then add up all the materials
requests they have received, and forward them to the
relevant sub-ministry. For example, a regional ministry may
have had requests for steel from factories producing cars,
razor blades, engineering tools, and refrigerators. Each one
may require various quantities of sheet steel, plate steel, and
bar steel, of varying thicknesses, qualities, and alloy
contents. The total requirement for the region is then
aggregated, and passed on to the sub-ministry, which then
aggregates all the regional requirements, and transmits them
to the central ministry. Total supplies are then calculated
and allocated by the supply committee, Gosnab; steel mills
are informed of the amounts of steel to be produced, and ore
mines and smelting works are told of their quota.

This may sound relatively simple and straightforward;
simple enough, despite the number of factors to be achieve-
able—difficult to administer, but possible. All that we have
really is an enormous state-controlled apparatus for the
collection and transmission of information; but too much
information for it to be possible to extend the process to
cover the whole economy. And far too much information
would be needed for the planners to attempt to include an
accurate assessment of the consumers' needs and wishes—or
to assess any changes in society.

Under the present system the planners calculate the

probably needs of the state and the consumers, estimate the likely changes in those needs, the probable changes in productive technology, and the degree to which such improvements would allow increased productivity. But a lot of changes can occur in five years. *"Economists in Eastern Europe and the U.S.S.R. long have recognised that, theoretically, a new long-term plan should be constructed each year, to incorporate the latest information about preferences and technology".*[1] Instead of a series of plans, say 1976-80, 1980-84, and so on, each year a new plan should come out, so the sequence would be 1976-80, 1977-81, 1978-82, etc. This is known as 'rolling planning', and would be far more efficient; but it has not been introduced because it is enough of a job to develop a five year plan in five years; to create one *every* year would be a mammoth task.

Thus, even to include the yearly changes in consumer requirements (or technology) would be too much for the planners; everything that the economy creates will be out of date even as it is introduced. And here one is talking not about personal preferences, but about consumer needs as assessed by Gosplan. What the rolling plan would be adjusted for would be Gosplan's opinions of consumer requirements, or Gosplan's decisions regarding what the consumer would be given. To obtain an accurate assessment of the wishes of every consumer, and incorporate the aggregated needs in the final plan, would require the creation of an entirely new chain of ministries, sub-ministries, etc., right down to a market research team in every district.

One suitable way of doing this would be by asking every consumer to give a full list of all the purchases that he or she would make in the coming year, or five years, detailing not

1. Wayne A. Leeman *Centralised and Decentralised Economic Systems*, Rand McNally.

only the items, but also the preferred characteristics of each item. For example, the colour, style, and quality of a pair of jeans; the size and texture of a loaf of bread; the flavour and strength of beer; and so on. But as the products considered become more sophisticated, there comes a point when the consumer is no longer qualified to describe exactly what he wants. He would know what he wants when he sees the choice available, but he cannot define it beforehand.

For example, in describing a hi-fi system, very few consumers would know exactly what design they would like the system to have. And even fewer would be able to talk knowledgeably about V/U meters, output (RMS) per channel, frequency response range, and dB noise levels. Even fewer still would be able to talk about quality in terms of by-pass filter design, transistor failure rates, or the life expectancy of switches.

The economy can respond to this in one of two ways; it can produce a small range covering the consumer's basic requirements, or it can produce as large a range as possible in the knowledge that each consumer will find one of the range to be just right for him. In a centralised, state-owned economy, which tends to judge goods by whether or not they are socially necessary, and has trouble coping with a mere 40,000 items, it is reasonable to assume they would take the first approach. Only in a capitalist economy which had a large number of independent, competing producers, would one find the latter method followed.

So it is clear that the centralised economy will not offer the consumer a wide range of choice. But is it at least efficient? That is, once it has made its decisions, will it convert those decisions into goods in the most efficient manner possible?

There are two aspects to efficiency—technology, and human beings. To take them in order, there are no indications that productive technology in the Soviet Union is comparable with that in the west, in fact, with the existing structure, Soviet technology will always be out of date. The inability to introduce rolling planning to adjust to changes in consumption, also means an inability to adjust to new technology. Even if the latest machinery is brought in from the west as soon as it is invented, it will not be until the advent of the next five year plan that the equipment can be fitted in to the production system. The plan is created round the existing capacity, and it cannot adjust to *any* change overnight. So even if the human beings who run the economy are doing their very best to modernise, the plant in operation will always be an average of two and a half years out of date.

It was stated previously that the command economy was simply an apparatus for the collection and transmission of information; but it is more than that; it is an organisation run by human beings. And in anything run by people, with policies chosen by people, human problems of one sort or another are bound to become apparent somewhere.

Not only can one expect senior planners to impose their opinions—which may or may not be valid ones—but one can also expect that intermediate staff would have their effect on policy making and implementation. The effect would not be so obvious, but it would be there. The intermediate staff, the ministers and enterprise managers, are the ones who collect and transmit the information, and although this may seem like a straightforward task, there is plenty of scope for human error—or interference.

At the beginning of this chapter it was asked, was it really a great advance to replace selfishness with general welfare as society's motivating force? On the surface it seems like a wonderful idea; selfishness is not the most admirable of human qualities, and to elevate it to being the motive force of the economy is a little like making megalomania the deciding factor in allocating political office.

But selfishness is a universal characteristic, one that

everybody has; but to varying degrees. Some people think *only* of themselves, some put themselves first, while some place only their major needs first, with the major needs of others second. The first two descriptions can definitely be called selfishness, but the third could be described as enlightened self-interest, something slightly different; something comparable to the motivating factor which western economists talk about. It is only the critics of capitalism who point out the presence of selfishness, and only the most extreme critics who claim it has been elevated to a position of being the official driving power.

Nonetheless, 'naked self-interest' is something which should be eliminated. It would not be possible to create a system in which selfishness played no part in any decisions, but it would be possible to create one in which the harmful effects of it were minimised. This would be a society in which everyone would be able to maximise his or her own welfare, and also, everyone would be constrained by other people's ability to maximise welfare. It would be a structure under which individuals who sought their own self-interest would be less likely to harm others than under existing systems, but more likely to directly or indirectly improve the welfare of others. In other words, a system which creatively channeled 'selfishness'. This does not apply to either monopoly capitalism or communism.

In both existing systems there is a hierarchy of power, and obviously those with the most power have the greatest opportunity to exercise their selfishness, to allow it to influence others. The majority of the population have little or no power, and should their drive be described as selfishness, they have no chance to exercise it. In fact, they have no opportunity whatsoever to safeguard their own welfare.

Under the command economy, those with the ability to look after their own interests will do so, and the only ones with the ability to do so are the administrators. Yet by doing no more than fulfilling their role in the system, and protecting their own interests, they distort the whole economy. Their role is to transmit information to the planners and policy makers; but is their real task to maximise the achievements of the plan, or to ensure that the plan will be fulfilled?

In other words, is their goal the general welfare of maximum output, or the safe selfishness of obeying orders? They are, after all, only civil servants, and if they offer optimistic predictions that later turn out to be unattainable, they lose face; they lose respect, promotion opportunities, and they may even lose their jobs. If they are to put in production figures that they intend to achieve, then they must put in underestimates, and err on the side of caution.

When the Soviet plan is drawn up, and production targets specified, each manager sends in an estimate of the target production level that he thinks he could achieve, and the quantity of materials, labour, fuel and so on that he will need to reach his target. To make sure that he can achieve the figure, he will probably underestimate the potential output of his factory, and overestimate the material input needed. There is often a bonus for fulfillment of the plan, ranging from 20% to 100% of the manager's salary. The Soviet authorities sometimes complain about managers' 'slavish adherence' to the plan, but there are not known to be any bonuses for overfulfillment of the plan. So if the factory produces less than, or more than it is committed to, the manager receives no bonus. It is obviously in his interest to underestimate what the factory is capable of, so that he has a margin of error in case of problems; that way he can be certain of reaching the planned output.

The same arguments apply with equal force to all the ministers who make up the intermediate links in the chain. They may or may not have bonuses, but they do have jobs and promotion prospects, and a little judicious adjustment of the aggregation figures would improve their chances of the plan being fulfilled in their area. For example, requests may have been put in for 100,000 tons of plate steel, 1,000,000 tons of sheet steel, and 700,000 tons of bar steel. It would be quite reasonable for the minister to put in an aggregate request for 2,000,000 tons of steel, thus allowing for any losses in converting the basic steel into the types and grades needed. But more important from the minister's point of view, is the greater probability of his region fulfilling its part in the plan.

It should be noted that once the plan has finally been determined, neither the factory manager nor the minister have any interest in significantly overfulfilling it, especially on any regular basis. Because if they consistently achieve more than they claimed they could, then the accuracy of their figures is put in doubt. To maintain credibility they must over achieve only rarely—often enough to give the impression of trying to maximise output, but not often enough to invalidate their own target levels.

So we have an arrangement which virtually encourages people to produce less than they are capable of. The remaining factors affecting efficiency include a rationally planned production system within the factory, factories being close to the optimum size, and transport costs being taken into account when locating factories. But there are no indications that any of these factors are treated rationally, nor is there any incentive to do so. Each of these items suggests innovation, and an educated quest for greater profitability. But how can there be innovation when the innovators are unlikely to benefit from it, and may even damage their promotion prospects? How can there by managers trained in profit-making, in a society which refuses even to recognise the concept of profit?

And these factors merely relate to technical efficiency,

which although important, is not the only consideration. A factory may have a technical efficiency of 100%, with a layout, machinery, and production processes designed to completely eliminate wastage of manpower, raw materials, or fuel. But if the human beings working in the factory are untrained, careless, lacking in motivation, incentive, or morale, then the theoretical efficiency will never be reached. The material conditions may be perfect, but if the needs and motives of people are ignored, then the system can never operate effectively.

The planners have no reason to improve efficiency; their goal is to construct a workable plan. The intermediate ministers and the enterprise managers have no incentive; their only task is to follow orders and fulfil the plan. Nor is there any point for the manager to try and reach the output level that the factory is capable of. Apart from fulfilling the plan, what benefits him is having a gap between planned output and potential output, so that he can guarantee getting his bonuses. Nor is there any inducement for the worker to improve productivity; pay is low, and much of what he might want to buy is not available.

No-one in the entire system has any encouragement to maximise production, widen the range of goods, or create goods that are what the consumer wants. So the consumer's interests are ignored, while the administrators and managers look after their own interests.

But if the system cannot produce effectively, can it at least produce accurately? In other words, can the state make, on behalf of the consumer, all the decisions that the consumer would otherwise have made for himself? To do this the state must correctly identify, locate within the plan, and fulfil all the decisions that otherwise would have been taken independently.

This would require total and accurate information on consumer tastes; in the U.S.S.R. they do not have the organisations necessary to collect such data, and it is unlikely that any centralised economy ever will have them. The collection and processing system needed would be so large and so complex, that by itself it would take up a significant proportion of the nation's labour and resources.

But supposing the consumer's decisions were somehow accurately gauged by planners who had a considerable instinct for popular needs, and that a valid and beneficial plan was derived from this instinct; would it then be possible to fulfil the plan correctly? According to Wilczynski, progress in mathematics and programming, with new high-memory computers, make it possible to solve planning problems involving billions of calculations in just a few hours. But as any computer programmer knows—GIGO—garbage in, garbage out.

Improved methods of calculation are irrelevant to the success of the command economy if the information mechanism is not accurate. And the data transmitted to the planners will remain inaccurate for as long as it is in the interests of the managers and administrators that it remain so. This is the opposite of the market economy, where it is in most people's interest for all data to be totally accurate. Their incomes depend on accuracy and adaptability.

This could be seen as a plea for selfishness, but is really a plea for enlightened and universally accessible self-interest. In the ideal free market, everyone should be able to seek their own self-interest, as long as it does not conflict with the needs of others. But the market is structured so that very often, when people seek to maximise their own welfare, it benefits others as well. The company that seeks more customers makes its prices lower; the company that wishes to expand its output looks for a consumer need that it does not yet satisfy; the company entering business looks for a need that *no* other company caters for. Everyone is trying to make money, but in doing so, they provide employment and consumer goods.

The command economy is structured so that only a minority can control their own welfare; but in seeking their own best interests, they harm the well-being of others. Power is concentrated in a few hands, but when those that have it, exercise it, there must inevitably be repercussions.

The command economy does not look after anyone's interests except the administrators. It does not, and could not have, the organisations for learning what the consumers want. The information mechanism that it does have is structured to encourage the use of false data. It cannot offer the consumer freedom of choice, nor does it offer a reasonable standard of living. Instead it creates a system of shortages, artificial prices, poor quality, and limited choice.

What little success it has depends on the elimination of one of Marx's major guidelines, and the re-introduction of market price mechanisms. For it to be more successful would require the complete elimination of Marx's proposals.

It is a system that offers authoritarian government and incompetent industry. Even within its own self-imposed limits, it is a failure. And over all this hangs the fact that the state owns the whole economy, indeed, the entire society. With this it creates a monopoly that is infinitely more powerful than any mere capitalist monopoly. It is the ultimate concentration of power; and therefore, the most dangerous.

6

The Real World

Russian Failure: Yugoslavian Success

In considering the real-life characteristics of communist society, it is of course very tempting to take Russia as one's example. Firstly, it is a very easy target to attack, being an obvious failure economically, socially, and politically. Secondly, it contains a complete catalogue of all the things that are wrong with traditional Marxist theory; it has low standards of living, an oppressive social system, and is a total dictatorship.

Some Marxists might object to the cliched use of Russia as a prize example of the faults of communism. But the fact is that Russia started out as a Marxist orientated system, and by adhering closely to the practical guidelines laid down by Marx, became the authoritarian state that it is today. And the U.S.S.R. will continue to be a justifiable target for attack until a) all communists reject the Soviet system in its entirety, and b) they admit that it has failed, and modify their theories to make sure that such things never happen again.

There is nothing whatsoever in Russian society that is beneficial, and even its few defenders can only offer the dubious claim that it has had to contend with many disadvantages. But on closer inspection it becomes apparent that these disadvantages were actually created by the system.

Following the revolution the government attempted to impose total control over the economy, and gradually introduced the centralisation and planning that were the forerunners of contemporary methods. But the planning was inefficient and ineffective, doing little but create shortages. The planners were working towards the Marxist goal of centralised administration, but neither Marx nor Engels had ever offered any practical advice as to how this would be achieved. So even the unsatisfactory system created by the planners was a major theoretical advance, but in practical terms it was just not good enough. This, coupled with the variety of ministries, often sending out conflicting orders, meant that the economy was gradually deteriorating, particularly in the industrial sector.

The agricultural sector was no better off. The administration of the central authority's edicts was often imposed by force, which did very little except create resentment. The supposed surpluses produced by peasant farmers was commandeered by requisition squads who became increasingly ruthless. There was no fixed definition of 'surplus', nor were the peasants paid for their produce, except on the occasions when they were paid in the almost worthless inflation-hit paper currency. So there was little incentive for the peasants to produce a surplus; or indeed, anything at all.

Between 1913 and 1921 agricultural production fell by 40%. Production of raw materials and basic commodities fell by as much as two-thirds—in the case of coal and oil—or by up to 95% as happened with steel.[1] In 1921 Lenin realised the futility of conflict with the peasants, and the ineffectiveness of central planning, and so he introduced a change of policy—NEP—the New Economic Policy. Confiscation of grain surpluses was replaced by a fixed tax on grain production, levied in kind; the peasants were then allowed to

1. Alec Nove *An Economic History of the U.S.S.R.*, Allen Lane.

sell their surplus privately, at whatever price they could get. In addition, the nationalisation of small-scale industry was revoked, privately owned factories with up to 20 workers could be formed, and state-owned factories could be leased by individuals or by co-operatives.

NEP was an enormous success. Agricultural output increased rapidly, the famines of earlier years were eliminated, and harvests were back to pre-war levels. But NEP was capitalism, for it to function properly required a free market—and both of these things were anathema to the Bolsheviks. As Stalin came to power he gradually reversed the new policies. In 1926 grain prices were reduced, taxes on high profits were introduced, surcharges were levied on the cost of transporting commercial goods, and high prices were made illegal—although not defined. Two years later grain prices were reduced again, and sales to the state fell by up to a third, as peasants turned to producing meat, bacon, and eggs instead. Then in 1930, private trade was condemned as speculation, and the employment of labour made illegal; NEP had ended.

It had put the Soviet economy back on its feet again, with industrial and agricultural production back to pre-war levels; but the price was the reversal of Marxist principles and the re-introduction of capitalism. What was needed, according to the leaders of the party, was a return to state ownership; but there were a number of ways in which this could have been achieved. Preobrazhensky advocated raising the prices of industrial goods, siphoning off some of the peasants new wealth, but without any overt or direct attack on their living standards. This would have encouraged the peasants to produce more grain, and allowed the state to accumulate capital.

Stalin's method was simpler; he took an armed force into the Urals, and requisitioned all grain considered to be surplus. Once Stalin's position within the party had been consolidated, this became the accepted method of grain collection. But the peasants did not co-operate, and so government powers were extended to include coercion, intimidation, fines, imprisonment, and the confiscation of property. This last item was used most widely against the kulaks, the more affluent peasants—although nobody could define exactly what a kulak was; or to put it another way, a kulak was anyone who Stalin or the requisition squads called a kulak. An estimated four million of these people had their property confiscated, and were then deported to the less hospitable regions of Russia, where many of them died. The remaining peasants were forced to join collective farms.

The coercion continued during the first Five Year Plan, covering 1929 to 1933, but this time it was justified by the need to fight against the merchants, the capitalists—and the kulaks. It was also claimed that the state had to fight against saboteurs and wreckers—the evil people who wished to destroy the heroic achievements of the communist revolution. But in many cases these people were simply engineers, economists, or administrators who had failed to achieve the tasks set for them, or perhaps disagreed with the goal or the methods of the Five Year Plan. These 'wreckers', including a number of prominent economists, were exiled or sent to concentration camps, where many of them died.

   Solzhenitsyn cites a number of examples of this policy in his book, *The Gulag Archipelago*. The most interesting of these involves Nikolai von Meck, an engineer who suggested increasing the load pulled by freight trains, and so raise the tonnage carried. The GPU—a predecessor to the KGB—decided that von Meck's real intention was to wear out the track and rolling stock by putting an excessive strain on it, and thus destroy the nation's transport system. He was accused of wrecking, and shot. The next Commissar of Railroads ordered the doubling or even tripling of freight loads, and when some engineers objected that this was too much, they were accused of being limiters; and were shot.

Because of centralisation, the imposition of collectives, the conflict between peasants and the state, and the eagerness to shoot dissenting experts rather than listen to their opinions, the Five Year Plan was a failure; living standards dropped dramatically throughout the whole period. Those who produced had no incentive to produce efficiently, the managers only course was to keep quiet and follow orders, and the planners had taken on a job that nobody had ever considered before; nor did anyone know if the job was even possible. To attempt to blame 'wreckers', peasants, or economists for the chaos that existed would be both irrational and inaccurate. The problem lay in the system itself, aggravated by the repressive atmosphere created by Stalin.

Many of the faults in the Soviet economy are directly attributable to the theoretical weaknesses of Marxism, but the chaos, famine, and oppression were the sole creation of the Russian leadership. The system was not suffering from unavoidable teething troubles; it was suffering from totally inappropriate policies, applied with blind ruthlessness. Stalin's achievement could be described as snatching defeat from the jaws of victory; the economy was growing again, conditions were becoming more liberal, people were co-operating with the state to build a new society; Stalin cancelled all that, irrevocably.

Stalin's reversal of NEP shows the stupidity of placing dogma above practicality or reason; a system that functioned well was replaced by one of unknown effectiveness, that later turned out to be a disaster. Perhaps Stalin believed that it was workable, but that does not justify the *way* in which he reverted to earlier policies. Stalin could have extended nationalisation, allowed leases on state factories to lapse, and manipulated prices; instead he used brute, authoritarian force.

The Russian economy has continued to be unsuccessful, as have the collective farms, and the centrally planned industrial structure. Despite record harvests in 1978, grain shortages continue; the U.S.S.R. regularly buys wheat from America, Canada, and Australia to make up the inevitable shortfalls in its crop. Grain imports over the years from 1973 to 1978 have cost the Russians more than $12,000 million. Collectives and state farms are now recognised to be the least efficient sector of Soviet agriculture; the peasants, using only 3% of the nation's farmland, produce 30% of the total agricultural output.

Nor is Russian industry in any better shape. Production of coal, gas, and steel frequently fall short of planned output, despite the fact that plans are often revised downwards. Plans are sometimes over-optimistic, frequently incomplete, and very often fall foul of shortages of equipment or machinery. Up till now Russia has been the world's largest oil producer, outside of the Arab nations, but due to shortages of drilling equipment they may become oil importers. Consumer goods are also scarce, affecting products from clothes, to bed-linen, to light bulbs; such goods as are available have to be queued for, and are usually of poor quality.

Because of its failure, Russia is a tempting target, and an easy one. But it is also a justifiable target because of the Marxist orthodoxy of its development. It has had a violent revolution, a repressive interim period of adjustment, and it has a centrally administered economy. The failings of Soviet Russia are the failings of Marxist theory.

The most crushing indictment of Russia—and of communism—is that offered by ex-members of the party, and sympathisers, people like Arthur Koestler, Richard Wright, and Andre Gide. Their experiences with communism—described in *The God the Failed*—show how cruelly the party uses people; and then disposes of them when they are no longer useful or ideologically acceptable. Richard Wright's biographical tale is the most poignant in the book; the author, a black American looking for a society free of racial bigotry, finds instead rejection and dis-illusionment. Those who actually visited Russia—like Gide and Koestler—found their faith in communism destroyed.

But despite all this, Russia is not a suitable subject for a critique of Marxism. It is not only unfair to select the worst example of an ideology, it is also an unsatisfactory method. One cannot prove the falseness of an ideology by carefully selecting its most unsuccessful application. The way to see how a set of beliefs function is by examining a typical example of its operation, to see how it normally works. The faults that exist under a typical communist government can then be ascribed to communism itself, and not to the psychological aberrations of some temporary and possibly misguided ruler.

And inasmuch as Russia is typical of Marxist orthodoxy, there is no need for a rigorous and exhaustive proof of the unhealthy condition of the Soviet society. Conditions in Russia are quite well known, but more to the point, there is no need to attack the practice because previous chapters have demonstrated the illogic of the theories; and if the theory is wrong one cannot expect a rationally functioning system in practice. It is equally wrong to say, the theory is alright, it just doesn't work in practice. If it doesn't work then the theory is wrong; it may be incomplete, inconsistent, or perhaps has simply failed to take account of human factors, but this only means that the theory as it stands must be altered or adjusted before it is usable. In other words, the theory is wrong. And if the theory *cannot* work, then it is garbage.

On the other hand, if Marx's original theories were incorrect, one can reasonably expect that subsequent Marxist theoreticians have seen the faults in the previous exposition, and have learnt from them. Equally, communist states set up after the Russian one will have learnt from their colleagues mistakes, and will have modified their practice. Thus, an analysis of a more recently formed communist society will not only relate to a more typical example, it will also demonstrate a more complete and final version of Marxist theory. The faults that exist in such a society will represent the irreducible minimum that can be achieved under communism.

For these reasons I have chosen to take Yugoslavia as the typical representative of modern communism. It is the healthiest, most stable of the existing socialist countries; it has its own unique structure, based on lessons learnt during the split from Stalinist Russia; and it may perhaps represent the ultimate development of communism.

To a large degree it is a market economy, which means that there is less to criticise; the centralisation of Marxist ideology has been much diluted, and so is correspondingly less unpleasant. At the same time, it is the market character-istics of the Yugoslav economy which give it its health; if the market sector spread any further, it would cease to be a socialist country. In fact, some people have objected that Yugoslavia is not a communist country; and the first person to make this claim was Stalin. But the dominant political organisation is the League of Communists of Yugoslavia, while the president, Tito, has been leader of the Communist Party of Yugoslavia since 1937. The ideology may not be pure, but it is Marxist.

From 1918 to 1941 Yugoslavia was dominated by the Karadjordjevic family, who owned most of the country's industry, and allowed the rest to be owned or run by foreigners. For example, in 1941 98% of the copper, lead, timber, and cement industries were owned by foreigners. But on March 25th of that year the Prince and the ruling government signed a pact allying Yugoslavia with Germany and Italy. There were massive demonstrations, and two days later the government was overthrown; ten days later, on April 6th, German, Italian, and Hungarian forces invaded the country. Throughout the war the only effective resistance movement was the communist National Liberation Army, led by Josip Broz Tito. Their numbers grew from 80,000 in 1941 to 300,000 at the end of the war, by which time the partisans were tying down 30 divisions of axis soldiers.

By the end of the war the old government and the royal family had been stripped of office and power, and the Council of National Liberation asked Tito to form a new government. In the elections of November 1945 an estimated 90% of the electorate voted for People's Front candidates, and for Tito as president. The country was declared to be a federal republic, and a new constitution was written, which came into force on January 31st 1946.

As early as 1942 the Yugoslavs felt ready to form a government, but Stalin opposed this. Tito had been in Russia during the 1917 revolution, and there is no doubt that he felt considerable sympathy for Russian views; so the Council of National Liberation was formed instead. Between 1946 and 1948 successive sectors of the economy were nationalised; at this stage Stalinist ideology was still dominant. But Stalin wished to impose a Russian style of social organisation—he wanted the Yugoslav Communist Party to play a major role in government, and he wanted to see collectivisation introduced. Under pressure from Stalin and the Cominform—the information agency for national communist parties—Yugoslavia introduced collectivisation.

But as in Russia, it was a failure; there was a serious decline in agricultural production, and the programme was abandoned in 1953. But Stalin's last criticism was even more unacceptable; he accused Yugoslavia of 'nationalism', which many saw as a demand that they end their claims for an independent internal development. Stalin wanted the country to follow his line of dogma; he wanted the Cominform and the Communist Party to have total control over all decisions. But the Yugoslavs sought not only an independent development, but a system that was acceptable to the broad political spectrum that ruled the country. They wanted a government that was run by Yugoslavians.

Stalin applied considerable pressure to ensure that his line was the one that would be followed. In 1947 half of Yugoslavia's foreign trade was with Cominform countries; by 1950 it was zero—all trade with Cominform had been suspended. So that year the separation from Cominform was made official, and Yugoslavia sought its own road to Marxism.

The principle of self-management was first put forward in 1949 when 215 companies were sent instructions on the formation of works councils. The following year the first law regarding self-management was passed, but the initial idea had already attracted some support, and a number of companies had sent requests for permission to form works councils. By the time the new law had passed the Federal Assembly there were already more than 500 works councils actually in operation.

The law proposed that works councils elect a managing board from its own members, and that one member of the board be elected director. The works council would make general policy decisions on running the company, and also had the right to distribute profits between investment or personal income, as it saw fit. The size of the council varied from 15 members to 120, depending on the size of the enterprise, but as there was just one council per company, in later years the system was regarded as representative rather than a direct democracy.

Additional changes were that the national plan ceased to state what each company should produce, and what price it should charge. Rationing and the compulsory purchase of agricultural produce was ended, and the peasants were allowed to sell what they wished at whatever price they could get. This liberalisation of the economy reduced prices, boosted sales, and led to the high growth rates of the fifties and early sixties.

It was around this time that another event occurred which may explain why some people are unaware that Yugoslavia is a communist country. In 1958 the communist party deliberately set out to 'de-emphasise' its role in Yugoslavian politics. That year the party was re-named as the Communist League of Yugoslavia, and at the part congress it denounced as dogma the idea that the communist party should have a permanent monopoly of political power. But although the party's role has been de-emphasised, there are no sure signs that its power has been reduced; it is the only political party, and its chairman is automatically a member of the Presidium, the collective head of state.

The 1963 Constitution extended the principles of self-management to all organisations, including hospitals, universities, and banks. All workers were given the right to elect their management, and decide on working conditions, income distribution, and the development of the organisation. Also, the post of director had to be opened to new candidates every four years. The existing director could re-apply, but if his record had been a poor one, or some of the new candidates had formal or practical business qualifications, then the enterprise would acquire a new director. So gradually the number of directors with formal qualifications increased.

In 1965 came yet another reform. Yugoslav goods were thought to be uncompetitive in the world market; prices were felt to be too high, and quality was too low. The economy was developing as a closed system, protected by customs barriers, export subsidies, and other protectionist measures. The subsidies were almost completely eliminated by the reform, and companies that wanted to import goods had to provide the necessary foreign currency themselves, by exporting. The effect of the reform was a general shake-up of the economy. All firms were obliged to improve efficiency, including political factories—those in areas of high unemployment, or areas that had given a lot during the war. Apart from the increase in investment, the most obvious effect of the reform was a drop in the growth rate, from 10% to 6%.

But despite the pressures towards high levels of investment, the actual levels are often still too low. The works council allocates profits to the wages fund or to the business fund, for wages and investment respectively. And very often the council allocates too much for income—because every worker wants to earn as much as possible—and too little for investment. Because of this the federal government has had to increase the tax on profits, and then re-distribute the resulting funds to be used for investment.

A study carried out over the years 1962-66 showed that only three companies had made no significant investment, but in five enterprises personal earnings were greater than the company's net income. The majority of firms put about a third of their net income into the investment fund. It is interesting to note that the enterprises which set aside a large amount of funds for investment were also the ones with above average levels of personal income; greater investment means greater efficiency, and so creates higher future earnings.

But workers who were aware of the importance of investment were still putting personal welfare first. Having created high historic levels of investment, they were naturally unwilling to leave the company, as they would forfeit all rights to the high incomes they had helped to create. Equally, works councils were reluctant to take on new employees, paying them high wages which were the benefits of the existing workforce's thriftiness. These two factors tended to severely limit the mobility of labour; no-one wanted to leave a firm with a high investment record, nor did that firm wish to take on new workers.

The latter of these two factors played a major role in aggravating Yugoslavia's employment problems. With private ownership of industry discouraged, there is little enough to stimulate the formation of new companies. Any worker who has an idea for a new product can form his own company—if that product can be made efficiently by a firm with up to 5 or 10 workers, depending on the region. But if a larger workforce is likely to be needed, then his only alternative is to persuade his own works council to take up the idea. He then has to convince fifty or a thousand people that his inspired piece of intuition is actually a potentially profitable idea; the committee, as it does anywhere in the world, duly kills the unknown idea.

Company expansion or the creation of new product lines are the only possible source of new jobs, but with both of these discouraged by structural tendencies of the economy, it is not surprising that Yugoslavia has had high levels of unemployment for many years.

On the other hand, it could be said that Yugoslavia has achieved the ideal in industrial democracy. Unlike Russia, the factories are not owned by the state, but by the commune —equivalent to a local council. And although the workers do not own the enterprise, they do have a great deal of control. All workers belong to the working collective, and this body elects the workers' council. The council has very wide powers, and its exact role is usually specified in the charter or statute of the enterprise; these will include passing policy plans, methods for putting plans into action, appointing the director and other executives, deciding the price, type, and output of goods, and deciding the actual structure of the self-management system.

The managing board is the executive arm of the workers' council, and members are elected annually from among the members of the council. It has relatively little independence; its main job is to put into action the decisions of the council. The board's only decisions on running the company are those allowed it by the charter; it may draw up plans, but only those suggested by the council.

The day to day running of the company is carried out by the director and a small staff of experts. They handle the administration, accounts, and decide on the machinery, processes, and materials to be used in the factory. Also, the director has responsibility for assessing the legality of the decisions made by the workers' council.

Thus, the system is run on the most democratic lines possible. The workers as a whole elect the council, and the council elects the managing board and the director; while in smaller companies the whole collective votes on who will be the director. So general policy is controlled by the workers, and daily routine is handled by someone who has been chosen by the workers.

But this is not all. In addition there may be—depending on the size of the company—workers' councils for each separate factory owned by the enterprise, a council for each department of each factory, plus a committee *and* a commission for each council. A large company may have as many as a dozen committees—and perhaps a dozen commissions. For example, the Sava enterprise in Kranj, Slovenia, has 13 collective executive bodies or committees; the committee for the enterprise programme and development; for the organisation of work and management; for production planning and quality; for financial and commercial affairs; for the distribution of income and personal earnings; for management of the social services and welfare fund; for employment and education; for work safety; for information; for vocational training; for assessment and compensation of damage and injury; for establishing dereliction of duty; and for internal arbitration.

The Jesenice iron and steel works of Jesenice, Slovenia, has a workers' council with 69 members, it has 12 commissions, 10 committees, plus a few collective executive bodies, sector commissions, and works unit councils. The Crvena zastava works in Kragujevac, Serbia, has 14 workers' councils, 15 managing boards, 19 departmental councils, and no less than 134 committees—plus some standing and *ad hoc* committees.

In attempting to create democracy they have created bureaucracy. In most countries the political system is either undemocratic or else is imperfectly democratic. Yet this is the sector where democracy should operate; it is the politicians who create the type of society we live in—the availability of education, health care, and housing, and the structure of the economy. Once the economic structure has been determined it should be possible to leave its operation to the individuals who run the companies. Democracy is a good general principle, but it is not a good idea to put everyone in charge of the day to day running of companies, schools, or hospitals.

It can be accepted that most workers will be sufficiently aware of peoples' requirements to know roughly what goods will sell, and may even have a vague idea of the price that should be asked. But the exact type of product is best left to product designers, experts in the technical specifications of that particular product. Similarly, investment decisions should be left to those with detailed knowledge of the state of manufacturing technology, and of the comparative costs of different processes. When commercial decisions are to be made, it is best to leave them to the experts; the design of a portable radio, or the price of an ingot of steel, are not things that are politically or socially important enough to justify bringing in an extra dozen or a hundred decision makers.

A more serious objection is that in allowing democracy to take control of the decision-making processes of a company or hospital, one is interfering with the effectiveness of the organisation's running. The more people are involved in a decision, the greater the time it will take. When an emergency patient is taken to a hospital it is not a good idea to convene a meeting of the surgeons, nurses, porters, and lab assistants to discuss what the treatment should be, if the patient should be operated on, and if so, by whom; and who should take the blood tests, who should decide which anesthetic to administer, etc, etc.

An organisation, whether its function is economic or purely welfare, should have jobs allocated to all its staff according to their skills and training, and the normal running of the organisation should require no more than that every member of the staff get on with his or her own job. Otherwise the organisation may be crippled by permanent democratic indecision; everyone will be so busy trying to decide who should be put in charge, what is the minimum percentage of the vote they should have to be elected, on what basis candidates should be chosen, and so on, that no-one would have any time for the actual running.

After the Portuguese revolution there was great concern that post-Salazar Portugal should be run democratically. The result was that for a whole year the entire economy was virtually immobilised while the workers discussed how to run things, how to structure the decision-making process, and so on.

In both Portugal and Yugoslavia the structure of the economy, or at least the types of ownership that are allowed, are already fixed by the government. The state has decreed that only the local commune can own a company, that workers, individuals, or groups may not own companies—above a certain minimal size. The workers are then allowed to democratically run the companies they are not allowed to own. This procedure is only democratic in a very limited sense; not only does it limit the worker's choice, it keeps him in the role of employee; the only difference is that instead of being employed by an individual, or group of individuals, he is employed by the community.

To a Marxist this may seem like the most democratic method possible, because according to Marxist principles, private ownership of any sort is anathema, it is the ultimate sin. Yugoslavia may be the most democratic of communist countries, but it still retains the basic Marxist distrust of capitalism, the distrust of anything owned privately and run for a profit. It is assumed that if an individual owns a company which he runs for profit, he will exploit the workers; the idea of a personally owned company run for profit, but *not* exploiting the workers is inconceivable.

The complex bureacracy set up to replace the owner/manager not only suggests a distrust of private capitalism, it strongly implies a distrust of the individual. Putting a committee in control of secondary management functions instead of a single expert, implies that checks and balances are necessary to restrain the behaviour of the individual. Perhaps in some fields a committee is a good idea, and provides a wider range of opinions on the subjects examined. But to have everything decided by committees is an unnecessary piece of bureacratisation.

On the other hand, it seems to be recognised that when fast and frequent decisions are needed, it is better to leave them to one person; that is presumably the reason why the companies are actually run by just one director. The works councils and committees are simply the necessary restraints to keep the director under control.

The distrust of private capitalism places Yugoslavia firmly in the main stream of Marxist thought, and at the same time clarifies one of the ultimate distinctions between Marxism and capitalism. A Marxist system may allow some forms of capitalism to exist, but only because it is the most efficient way to produce and distribute goods. It will then impose some form of artificial constraint on the system to ensure that people behave in a socially acceptable manner. Communists do not consider it possible for a form of capitalism to exist which contains its own built-in system of checks and balances; for example, the perfect competition economy. The attitude is that where capitalism exists it must be controlled by externally imposed restraints; the checks inherent in capitalism are not considered valid; it must be controlled directly by organisations, rather than accept the indirect control of market mechanisms.

As it is, Yugoslavia has rejected the Russian-style state ownership, and has disposed of the traditional Marxist command economy. If the complex management system were also eliminated, the resulting economy would be little short of pure capitalism. Excluding the social ownership, the self-management system is the only real Marxist feature of the economy; it is also the second major fault of the system.

When an individual owns and runs his own company, any decisions he takes are his, and his alone. He takes full responsibility for every aspect of company policy, and if anything goes wrong, he takes all the blame. In a large company, with its board of directors and hired experts, things are not quite so clear cut; policy selection becomes a group decision, and it is not quite so easy to apportion blame. But it is still one separate group that takes decisions, one group that has responsibility. With self-management, things are not so simple.

According to Milojko Drulovic, the problem of personal responsibility has caused a lot of discussion in recent years; the responsibility of the self-management groups, and of the executives. One problem is that an individual can be held accountable for his actions, but a collective can not. The works council can only be held responsible politically; the council may have to explain and justify its actions, or it may be removed from office, but it cannot be sued or indicted.

Drulovic says that, *"It is more often the case that enterprise directors and expert executives are, in fact, to blame, but are not obliged to bear any consequences: they take cover behind decisions of the workers' council . . . or the . . . loopholes of the internal enterprise regulations . . . It is not all that unusual for the workers' council to pass decisions simply as a matter of form, everything having been decided, in fact, by the director and expert executives, for whose work the council merely provides a 'cover'"* So if anything goes wrong, the directors blame the workers' council because the council passed the decision, and once it was passed, the directors had to carry it out.

Thus, even if the directors have initiated a policy, they can still blame the council; as the council must pass all decisions, it is responsible for all decisions. Drulovic implies that in practice the executives take the blame according to the degree of independence they have; if they put forward the proposals, and run the company almost as if it were their own, they must take full responsibility.

But what is true in reality may not be sufficiently obvious in day to day practice for the directors to be considered even politically liable; and it may be utterly impossible to hold them legally accountable. A good 'meetings man' will learn how to phrase problems so that someone will come up with a suitable proposal. The managing board of the enterprise meets once a week, and this is often enough for the director to plant ideas in the councillors' minds—ideas that the director considers worth trying, but perhaps is a bit of a gamble. He then waits until the council formalises the idea as a proposal. So if the idea goes sour in practice, the director is not blamed.

There will be a number of situations like this, where although the executives have a high degree of independence, their personal responsibility will not be sufficiently obvious for them to take either political or legal blame. And where responsibility is not clear cut, more irresponsible decisions will be taken.

The fact that nobody owns the enterprise is the real cause of the lack of accountability. Drulovic refers to a recent Congress of Worker-managers where one speaker gave the definition of social ownership as being everybody's and nobody's. When the benefits were being shared, everybody claimed ownership rights; when blame was being allocated, nobody owned it.

Among the most important of the defining characteristics of genuine ownership are risk, control, and legal rights; the risk of losing ownership, and the resultant care in one's use; the power to control one's property, and the resulting benefits; and the legal rights to income or the sale of the property. With social ownership both control and legal rights are diffuse and uncertain; and nobody bears any risk.

When people do not own the property they are dealing with, it is not unnatural to expect they will take less care of it than they would with their own property. Perhaps some individuals might be equally careful, but we are not dealing with individuals, we are dealing with large groups, and we cannot expect even a majority to behave as if they are the personal owners of the company. For each member of the workforce, his or her opinions are just one voice among many; there will be no feeling of control, and therefore, no feeling of ownership. At best the worker will feel like an involved team member, and at worst he will regard himself as just another employee. The effect of working for a large company is not unlike the alienation that Marx described as being unique to capitalism; but alienation comes from an impersonal atmosphere and a lack of control over one's life; and these can exist even under socialised ownership.

The inability of a firm to recognise each worker's individuality is a function of the company's size, not of its ownership structure. The more workers a company has, the harder it is for the company to recognise the work, the ability, the individuality of each and every worker. And the less a person's individuality is recognised, the less it can be expressed; therefore, working for a large company actually reduces a person's uniqueness. The worker-management structure may lessen this effect, but it cannot eliminate it. A considerable number of the workers may feel this alienation; they will not really feel like part of the company, nor will they feel like owners. And their decisions will be influenced by their attitudes; they will be less concerned about the stability of the company, about its investment capacity, or about its long-term health. As mentioned earlier, in a number of companies, wages received a higher proportion of funds than was good for the company, despite the fact that reduced levels of investment also reduced wage levels in the long term.

On the other hand, there would be workers who regard the company as merely a source of employment. Their attitude would be one of excessive caution when considering new products. Anything new is always a risk—demand is unknown, sales are unpredictable, so any money invested could be lost. And as the workers would be investing money that is potentially theirs, they are going to be very cautious in what they do with it. In the long term this means that new products or technologies will be slow to appear in Yugoslavia; the collectives would tend to wait until more adventurous companies had introduced the products, or until they had been tried out in other countries. Because of this, Yugoslavia will always be slightly behind most other developed nations, both in technology and in consumer goods. Productivity will tend to be lower, and imports will tend to be higher than would have been the case with a more adventurous system.

But whether the workers feel like pawns, cogs in the machine, or simply like employees, it can be certain that none of them feel or act like owners. They will not have the same sense of getting out what they personally put in, they will not experience the achievement of seeing all their ideas put into action, nor will they feel that they control the company's destiny. Each individual worker may be brimming over with inspirations regarding the manufacturing process, or possible new products. But there is always the awareness that new ideas have to be sold, pushed through the committee. And that knowledge itself would kill many new ideas; the effort of convincing other people of the idea's value is more than the idea is worth.

Although not all Marxist countries have self-management, the concept of private ownership of industry is banned or limited in all of them, to one degree or other. So although other countries wouldn't have alienated workers voting on investment levels, they would still have alienated workers. If the workers cannot own, then they are tied to whatever factory employs them; they can never be independent. For each country there is only one employer, and the worker is tied to that employer for the rest of his life. Even if the employer, and the type of Marxism, is as benign as that of Yugoslavia, it is still a less than ideal prospect. No matter what generous assumptions we may make about possible alternative forms of communism, there are still certain basic irreducible features. The worker, who does not own the company, will be one of a faceless team employed by people who also do not own the firm; few of them will ever be allowed to have their own company, and their ultimate employer, the state, is the only possible employer.

There is no doubt that Yugoslavia's economic structure is more beneficial than those of most other socialist countries. The best way to categorise the different types of structure is by the form of control exercised over the business sector. In

Russia power is centralised, external to the firm, and of greater magnitude than the company's power. In Yugoslavia power is decentralised, internal, and the restraint system is of roughly equal magnitude to the traditional decision-making sector. The Yugoslavian structure is definitely the best of the two, but it still leaves the worker, the average person, with very little control over his own life.

If the employer were anything other than the state, any self-respecting Marxist would instantly condemn the whole set-up as alienating and exploitative. And that is exactly what it is. The exploitation is not the crude variety of the nineteenth-century capitalist, but it is there just the same. By its very nature communism must be imposed on the entire country, taking in sympathisers, neutrals, and enemies alike; so people who strongly disapprove of the system are forced to work for it, pay taxes to it, and buy its produce.

As a rule, the lack of economic freedom is accompanied by a lack of political freedom and mobility. This partly explains why communist nations tend to be very repressive; they need the greater degree of force to keep dissidents in line, to prevent any reaction against the establishment. But in the case of Yugoslavia a more likely explanation would be the divisions within the country. As a visiting statesman put it, *"Six republics, five nations, four religions, three languages, two alphabets—one state!"* The problem in Yugoslavia is not the repugnance of the economic system, but the instability of the nation-state.

It is made up of the republics of Serbia, Croatia, Bosnia, and Macedonia, plus the autonomous provinces of Kosovo and Vojvodina. The problem is that economic development has been uneven throughout Yugoslavia, and Kosovo is one of the least developed areas, with a per capita income that is one third the national average. Unemployment rates can reach 60%.

The bitterness this can cause has been aggravated by the fact that 67% of Kosovo's population are Albanian, a group that has traditionally been exploited by the powerful Serbian minority. Albanian nationalism is a major force in Kosovo, but as the province borders onto Albania it is seen as a threat to Yugoslav security; a threat which the state has responded to by imprisoning anyone who demonstrates for Albanian nationalism, or who claims that Albanians are discriminated against.

Inexplicably, the urge for separatism is even stronger in Croatia; the region has a high per capita income, and no history of exploitation. But there are a number of separatist groups, some very active, right-wing—and violent. But most groups are non-violent, and the state's reaction has often been excessive. Although the Constitution of 1974 guarantees freedom of speech, the Penal Code still has *"articles which prescribe imprisonment for the non-violent exercise of freedom of expression"*.[1]   During the year July 1977 to June 1978 Amnesty International had been working for 86 political prisoners; and there are believed to be 200 political prisoners in Yugoslavia's jails.

Undeniably the state's response to dissidence or nationalism can be harsh and repressive; and it is able to wield this force because although officially most decision-making is decentralised, in practice the federal state still has a great deal of power. The state is always the repository of ultimate power, and this is particularly true of communist nations. And the workers have relatively little power; they are supposedly the owners of the means of production, but in many ways they are no more than employees. They depend on the state for their continued livelihood, but have no opposing power to wield against the state.

The localisation of ownership appears to have had only

1. Amnesty International Annual Report 1978.

marginal effects in reducing the power of the state, or increasing the power of the workers. The self-management enterprises receive their creation and their legitimacy from the federal government, and by implication, could have that legitimacy withdrawn at any time. This is not to say that such a withdrawal is likely, merely that it seems to be of greater probability than would be the case in a western nation.

Yugoslavia is a country whose political structure is still unfixed. It is on its fourth Constitution since the war, and constitutional amendments are almost as frequent. It has been said that the power of ministers and executives in the various regions depends not on their official position, but on their ease of access to the president. Power structures are not formalised, and are certainly not rigid. Perhaps in Yugoslavia's case this is a good thing, but in view of the vulnerability of communist nations to dictators, it must give rise to concern.

At best the workers has more influence over his environment than he would in a traditional communist society; but he does not have control, he is not able to live his life absolutely as he wishes. He is not able to choose his political system, or his political party; he cannot decide the structure of the economy, or the size of the business units; he cannot decide who should own the company that employs him, he cannot seek an alternative employer, and except for certain restricted cases he cannot form his own company, nor can he work for a privately owned company.

Marxism aims to liberate the worker from the capitalist, but instead makes him dependent on the state. The worker has not been freed in any way, he has simply exchanged one master for another. The power of the capitalist has been eliminated, and the power of the state has increased; the power of the individual, whether worker or not, depends entirely on the benevolence of the state. If the state is benevolent, as it is in Yugoslavia, it is almost a matter of luck; it is certainly not an inherent feature of Marxism.

As can be seen from the example of China, how a Marxist society is run depends not on the needs of the population, but on the opinions of the rulers. The way Yugoslavia was run was greatly influenced—some say dominated—by Tito; and this in itself would indicate the extent to which power is centralised, as it is under all communist governments. Yugoslavia has developed a decentralised economic and political system, and a strong democratic tradition; yet the way it is run after Tito's death may depend not on the wishes of the people, but on the opinions of Tito's successor.

Even the most democratic communist country of all may, one day, become just another dictatorship. And even though it is economically the most successful of all Marxist states, it still suffers from problems that are actually caused by its Marxist principles, ones that are at the very foundations of Marxist theory. Capitalism is evil, therefore it must be constrained; and constraint means interference, which means inefficiency.

Yet the Yugoslavian restraint of social ownership is almost the lowest level of interference that can occur. To improve efficiency further would require free market capitalism, with restraint being exercised only to ensure the fulfillment of social objectives; for example, establishing minimum income levels, low unemployment rates, pollution control, and so on. Remaining social objectives would be handled directly by the government, without any interference in the behaviour of policies of business.

Such a system would be remarkably similar to Scandinavian 'socialism', which is basically a free market, with only a nominal percentage of state ownership. Zarko Papic describes self-management as being a process rather than a completed system; if this is true, then one logical route for the process would be to eliminate interference in company policy-making, and for the government to take on the control of social objectives. In other words, company directors would make policy decisions as they saw fit—within given legal limits—and the state would make sure that social needs were cared for. It would be Marxist morality—which in most cases is merely a re-phrasing of earlier religious ethics—with capitalist economics. The final development of Marxism would result in the total evaporation of all signs of Marxism.

But self-management as it stands is undoubtedly harmed by the desire to keep capitalism under control, the wish to compensate for the evils of the profit motive. Unnecessary structures and bureaucracies are created, merely to perform functions that occur naturally in the free market. To call it clumsy is not the greatest accusation one could level against an ideology. But when the system concerned is the best that that ideology can offer, 'clumsy' is not a weak insult, but damnation by faint praise.

As was shown in earlier chapters, Marxist theory is inherently unsound—irrational, contradictory, and totally at variance with the facts. It should not be surprising that the practice, based on that theory, is also unsound.

7

The Heir of the Dogma

Modern Developments in Marxism

Throughout the last century there have been a multitude of social upheavals, most of them in complete opposition to the pattern of change predicted by Marx. So modern Marxists have had to adjust accordingly, and in the last few years new forms, new theorists and theories have appeared; and new dogmas.

In Britain, the most common form is socialism, as practised by the Labour Party. In this variant the communist takeover has been given a more electorally palatable description, with Clause 4 of the Labour Party's manifesto calling for 'common ownership' of the important sectors of the economy. What this really means is nationalisation; the Labour Party has no interest whatsoever in genuine common ownership, and only uses such phrases to give its policies a more egalitarian tone. Their aims, according to Tony Benn and others, are the nationalisation of all banks, insurance, property companies, etc; all the major strongholds of capitalism.

But as has surely been shown by the examples of British Leyland and British Steel, nationalisation is an excellent recipe for corporate disaster. BL is a government-inspired hybrid that, in its original separate parts, was responsible for over half the UK's motor industry's sales; in its present form it has managed to achieve a low of only 15 per cent. Its other achievements include the total inability to introduce a new mass-selling car to replace the Mini—introduced in 1959—and the TR7, a hardtop sports car, aimed at the American market, where convertible sports cars sell like hot cakes; and hardtops sell like cold tea. In February 1980 the then boss of Leyland, Michael Edwardes, said that smaller companies like BL could not match the high levels of investment made by the bigger multinationals. This was shortly after receiving a £300 million grant from the state, and refers to a company that was once half the British motor industry.

British Steel's achievements are equally underwhelming. So here is the news—taken chronologically from the newspapers of February 1980. On the 13th The Guardian reported that a Liverpool University economist, Richard Pryke, had suggested a complete break-up of BSC into its component parts. He attacked its planning, investment, and export policies, and expressed astonishment that throughout the massive cuts in BSC's workforce, there had been hardly any reduction in white-collar staff. On the 17th The Sunday Times ran an article by a BSC manager, condemning the decision to invest in low grade steel plant at a time when new producing countries were entering the low grade market; criticising British Steel's poor salesmanship; and condemning the patronising and pessimistic way in which the workforce had been informed of the company's prospects. And on the 20th, Sir Charles Villiers, chairman of British Steel, was reported as saying that £41,000 per year was not enough to attract good top management.

This is a sample of the policy that the Labour Party is offering. But they have also failed in other areas, most notably in their unwillingness to introduce a wealth tax. But a fuller list includes their *"failure to redistribute more radically the £1,200 million spent on providing mortgage tax relief . . . failure to end the tax relief on public schools or to stop diplomatic and defence staff sending their children to them on taxpayers' funds; a failure to repeal sexually discriminatory taxation laws; mere token expenditure on helping racial minorities; and only the most marginal improvement in providing community care for the mentally ill, the mentally handicapped and the elderly".* [1]

In Britain at least, socialism is in a sorry state, with its egalitarian policies forgotten, and its major platform being a discredited blunder based on an outmoded dogma.

Communism itself, strong in France and Italy, is waning in the UK. The C.P.G.B.'s figures for 1977 show just over 20,000 members, but in the election of 1979 the party only polled 16,800 votes; just 0.1% of the total cast.

The only facet of Marxism that is growing, attracting new converts, is the Marxism of Gramsci. Antonio Gramsci acquired his early ideas from the works of Croce, Salvemini, Papini, and other Italian writers, and for many years his views were strongly influenced by them. This gave him a view of change as being something that is made by men, not predetermined by a fixed historical pattern; change led by an intellectual elite, with the masses following. As neither Salvemini nor Croce were sympathetic to the forms of Marxism existing at that time, Gramsci too tended to regard Marx's work as little more than an intellectual curiosity.

After winning a scholarship to Turin University—along with fellow Sardinian, Palmiro Togliatti—Gramsci struck up a friendship with one of the professors, Umberto Cosmo. Gramsci and Cosmo shared a respect for the ideas of Croce and Salvemini, but Cosmo also persuaded his young protege to study the works of those who had inspired Croce; among them being Hegel. His subsequent conversion to socialism was actually the work of a fellow student, Angelo Tasca,

1. Malcolm Dean in *The Guardian*, January 28, 1980.

who devoted considerable effort to convincing Gramsci of the value and ideals of socialism.

But it was not until two years after joining the Italian Socialist Party (PSI) that Gramsci started a serious study of Marxism, this time encouraged by the professor of philosophy, Pastore. After leaving university he spent much of his time writing articles for left-wing journals such as Avanti, Sotto la Mole, and Ordine Nuovo—this last paper being financed by Tasca.

Through the PSI Gramsci became involed in the factory councils, and subsequently became aware that the existing trade union structure was not representing the workers democratically, was not taking sufficient note of what the workers themselves wanted. Gramsci attended meetings, and gave speeches, gradually converting the councils into educational centres, and a means for raising the workers' socialist consciousness.

But throughout these years, most of his writings were concerned with purely topical issues, immediate policies, and personalities of the day. What was lacking was an overall analysis of Marxist theory, as applicable to twentieth century Italian capitalism, or capitalism and revolution as general categories. What he needed was to distance himself from the minor trials and tribulations of the various groups, to stand back and consider what had to be done, what made a state vulnerable, or what made a social system beneficial.

In 1927 he was tried for attempting to overthrow the state by force; he was found guilty, and spent the rest of his life in prison. This, ironically, was just what was required—to allow his theoretical work to develop. Gramsci had never been particularly healthy, and eventually the stress of prison life was to kill him. But it also gave him the time to develop his ideas and create his greatest theoretical work.

The whole of Gramsci's thinking had been affected by his experience in the Turin factory councils, which made his attitude to social change a much more pratical one than that of many Marxist writers. Indeed, one of his central themes was the unity of theory and practice—or in Marxist terminology, praxis. Revolution demanded emotional commitment and a coherent theory, a theory grounded in practical and workable strategy. The concept of praxis eliminated any division between theory and practice; theory guides action, and action depends on the dictates of theory.

Gramsci's work in the factory councils also moved him away from the elitist ideas of Croce and Salvemini, the view that the intellectuals teach and lead, while the masses follow and obey. His contact with the workers presumably taught him that they have needs and wishes apart from the ones that the intelligentsia had managed to predict from a distance. The workers also have a wide variety of opinions, some of which may be more accurate than those of their teachers. But still, they needed to be taught Marxist theory, and Gramsci developed the concept of the 'organic intellectual', a person who lived and worked with the masses, who were a part of their culture, and who understood their needs. The 'organic intellectual' would teach the workers what had to be done, teach them the philosophy of Marxism, and the faults and vulnerability of capitalism. But they were no longer just teachers and leaders; they were also pupils.

Gramsci believed that the factory councils were more than a discussion centre, that they could provide the core of the impending social change. *"The revolutionary process takes place on the terrain of production, in the factory, where the relations are those of oppressor to oppressed, of exploiter to exploited . . ."*[1] *"The existence of the councils gives the workers direct responsibility for production, leads them to improve their work, institutes a conscious and voluntary discipline, and creates the psychology of the producer, the creator of history".*[2]

1. cited by Carl Boggs *Gramsci's Marxism*, Pluto Press.
2. cited by Carl Boggs, op. cit.

This change of attitude will ultimately bring about the *"elaboration of the forms of economic life and professional technique proper to communist civilisation"*.[1]

Thus, Gramsci was proposing a gradual change, a learning process combined with growing self-awareness and responsibility. Slowly, the workers' determination to control their own lives grows, the number and size of the factory councils expands, until finally they take over the factories and even parts of the state administrative system.

Gramsci's vision is very appealing, and is reminiscent of the worker control in Yugoslavia; but with one important difference. At the end of the war a communist government took power in Yugoslavia, and later created the factory councils. Gramsci assumes that the councils themselves will take power, aided by the trade unions and the party, but offers no detailed explanation as to how this will occur. He admits that *"we have not yet formed a tactical conception which can objectively ensure the creation of that state"*.[2] In other words, he doesn't know how it can be done.

Given that the capitalists own the factories, and will continue to do so until those factories are brought from then, or nationalised by a communist government, then the capitalists will continue to control the factories. The limited control over the productive processes that would be allowed by the most enlightened capitalist—for example, the worker directors in Germany—leaves the ownership structure unchanged. The shareholders are still the technical owners, and the company executives still have the last word in control.

There is no way that a gradual expansion in worker self-determination and awareness can create a transfer of ownership, either the legal ownership via shares, or the

1. cited by Carl Boggs, op. cit.
2. Cited by Alastair Davidson   *Antonio Gramsci*, Merlin Press.

factual equivalent of total control. Given the political system that exists, there is only a certain amount of control that the workers can take by agreement or negotation; if they wish to go beyond that, they must use force; which promptly makes their actions illegal. A communist government could offer a powerful backup to the factory councils, allowing them to press their demands much harder; but Gramsci believed that the factory councils would create the revolution, therefore, one can not postulate a situation in which the councils can succeed only after the revolution has taken place.

Considering the implausibility of the councils achieving social change, and Gramsci's failure to detail how such a change would occur, his emphasis on praxis seems a little hollow. If praxis is the unity of theory and practice, then it must take account of what is possible; and it must plan for specific methods of realising that possibility. A theory of praxis which ignores pragmatism is not only a bad theory; it is also not praxis.

But Gramsci was practical enough to realise that Marx's idea of an inevitable revolution was unrealistic. As Boggs points out, in one fell swoop, the Bolshevik revolution of 1917 repudiated all the laws of Marxist determinism. If a revolution could occur outside the prescribed pattern, then one could operate inside the historical framework—and not have the predicted result. The laws had failed; therefore, new explanations were needed.

Apart from their obvious inaccuracy, Gramsci also disapproved of the deterministic laws on purely strategic grounds. If people thought that the revolution was inevitable, depending only on the inherent contradictions of capitalism, then they do not need to do anything to bring about the revolution. It will come of its own accord, automatically. The only purpose in joining the Communist Party is to show solidarity; no practical purpose is served by it, the rate of social change is not accelerated, the pre-determined pattern of the future is not changed. Because quite simply, it cannot be changed. Such thinking, argued Gramsci, can only bring apathy and a lack of initiative, and ultimately would only harm the communist cause. What was needed was a strong emphasis on the failure of historical determinism, and on the need for the individual to help create the revolution. This latter item Gramsci provided, through his theory of the factory councils.

But what was more important was explaining why the laws had failed. If the laws were totally invalid then Marxism had nothing to offer as a scientific system; if the laws were only partially correct then an explanation was needed as to what particular aspect of society had been overlooked. Possibly the laws could be modified in the light of experience, or perhaps they would be jettisoned altogether; but from Gramsci's point of view, Marxism could never again claim scientific infallibility.

"With unassailable logic, he observed that the objective conditions for socialist revolution (i.e. alienation and exploitation in capitalist society) had existed in Europe for several decades, but nowhere had there been a revolution". [1]

The traditional Marxist explanation was the existence of state power, coercion, the ability of the state to dominate its subjects, and force them to behave in the way the state required. But it was an unsatisfactory explanation; it ignored the fact that the state apparatus never had total control, and rarely used what power it did have. And it was a particularly dismal answer when dealing with the supposed crisis of capitalism, a time when the system would be even more vulnerable than usual to attacks from within. A crisis of capitalism implies both economic and social instability, with widespread uncertainty as to the correct remedies, and

1. Carl Boggs *Gramsci's Marxism*, Pluto Press.

therefore, uncertainty as to which group should be in office. At such a time, Marxists should be able to take power merely by stating that they had predicted the crisis, and had already worked out the appropriate cures.

But things had not happened that way; so there had to be something outside the normal reasoning of crises, coercion, and revolution. Gramsci's answer was that there are two types of coercion—the physical coercion as supplied by the military and judiciary, and ideological coercion. The state had direct or indirect control over a broad range of opinion-forming organisations—schools, the press, the church, and even trade unions. The state's beliefs were promoted through these various mouthpieces literally from birth to death, and such dominance over the opinion-forming apparatus meant—at the very minimum—that peoples' ideas would be influenced by the prevailing beliefs. A more likely outcome would be that many people would be totally convinced by the establishment view.

Gramsci believed that this was the crucial form of manipulation; the control of ideas and opinions so that people would actively support the system, giving it the assitance it needed in the period of crisis. In approving of its values, they approve of its continuing existence, and so will aid it in time of crisis, or work against anything that threatens it.

The normal Marxist explanation, when a crisis of capitalism failed to induce the predicted revolution, was that this was not *the* crisis. But this is no more than an after-the-event excuse, a post-failure apology, typical of the unfalsifiability of Marxism described in Chapter 2. If there was a *the* crisis, then it must be describable and definable, it must be unique in some way that separates it from merely passing crises. Therefore, it must be possible to state absolutely beforehand whether or not it is *the* crisis.

In Gramsci's view there was no *the* crisis, there was no

inevitable revolution; the failure occurred because the workers had been so indoctrinated by the organs of the system that they actually helped it through the crisis. The crucial factor was not physical force, but cultural persuasion; or in Gramsci's terminology—ideological hegemony. The whole of the workers' lives had been dominated by the organisations, culture, and ideas of the establishment, and to expect them to jettison their acquired beliefs in a single period of instability, and take up a socialist consciousness, was just not rational.

What was needed was a gradual replacement of the indoctrinated attitudes by a socialist awareness, guided by the teachings of the organic intellectuals, and by the new understanding and self-confidence gained in the factory councils. There would be an interim period of cynicism and uncertainty about the prevailing ideas, but gradually, the old views would be replaced by a new ideology. There would be a socialist consciousness, based on a socialist philosophy, with new culture, values, life-styles, and even new art-forms —literature, poetry, painting, etc.

The new society would have all the forms and attributes of a culture in the widest sense, but with a different economic basis. The process would be gradual and total, with economic reform linked inseparably with intellectual reform. The revolution would not be a single act or event, but a continual process, with the transformation of the economy accompanied by the gradual change in attitudes.

A communist society would be the last stage of that process, after the factory councils had taken over the administrative functions of the state, and the old capitalist hegemony had been replaced by the new ethos, the integrated culture. And so, one more aspect of traditional Marxism has been disposed of. Instead of Marx's *"the class struggle necessarily leads to the dictatorship of the proletariat"*, with its *"forcible overthrow of all existing social conditions"*, i.e., a revolution followed by a transitional phase, we have no revolution, but a gradual progression instead. There is a slow change that is utterly unlike the dictatorship phase proposed by Marx, and described by Lenin. It is a process rather than a separate stage; it is the existence of change instead of a period of adjustment to a change that has already occurred.

But as has been shown, it is unreasonable to assume that the factory councils, whatever their structure or level of democracy, could take over the ownership and control of the factories, or the administrative functions of the state. But Gramsci states that the economic change and the ideological change go hand in hand; so perhaps if the councils cannot take power, there will be no change in attitudes either. This however, would be an unfair and over-literal interpretation of Gramsci's view; values can be changed in a variety of ways; but there is no reason to believe that any of these ways might lead to socialism.

The factory councils are precisely that; councils based in the factories with a membership comprised of the workers themselves. Therefore, any transformation of values that occurs takes place after the individual has reached sufficient age to be a worker. That is, the councils must change the beliefs of people who have been through the state education system, have been subjected to at least some degree of the church's teaching—which in Italy is considerable—and must unavoidably have heard at least a modicum of the establishment's views, as promoted by the mass media. It is not an overwhelming disadvantage, but nor is it an equal contest because the councils are starting later in the process than the state.

The contest is also unequal in numbers. The factory councils, possibly with the aid of the party and the trade unions, are fighting the combined ideological power of the government, the education system, the mass media, the church, bureaucracy, and big business. The odds are not good. But the prospect would be made considerably more attractive if there were any guarantees of the truth or eventual success of the struggle.

But there are no guarantees. Even if the party and the councils managed to discredit the established values, it would not mean that the people would automatically turn to socialist values. Simultaneously with the growth of the factory councils, Gramsci was fighting a losing battle against fascism, progressing from 1920 when he regarded fascism as nothing but an illegal terrorist organisation, to 1927, when the fascist government of Mussolini imprisoned him.

The values that people hold do not only depend on the intellectual teachings and rationality they are offered. For less educated people—like the peasants and workers of Italy in the 20s—values depend a good deal on the emotions. And fascism, whatever the era, is a force that appeals to the raw, basic emotions. Gramsci recognised the disadvantage he was at, and sought ways to combat it; but he was an intellectual, not a demagogue, and the fight between idealism and simplicity was not an equal one.

In losing the political battle, Gramsci also lost the theoretical one, because although fascism had no theory, its political victory meant that Gramsci's theory had failed. He had proposed a method of fighting the ideological hegemony of the state—of which fascism was a crude variation—and failed; he had claimed that one could create a communist society by giving the workers a socialist awareness, and been defeated.

But perhaps Gramsci's failure was not in his theory, but in his inability to recognise the immense strength of the existing value system, and its political ally, fascism. The question then becomes, could Gramsci's methods work in modern Italy—or indeed, any other country? Gramsci's proposal was struggle between one value system and another, hence, as all philosophies have a degree of emotional appeal, the crucial factor in the long term would be the validity of its intellectual content. If his blue-print was not scientific, then it would be unlikely that any party basing its programme on his strategy could ever come to power.

Here the prospects are even bleaker. Gramsci rejected the 'scientific' laws of Marx, saying that the laws of the physical sciences are totally inapplicable to the social sciences; they cannot hope to attain the same precision as they deal with completely different phenomena. Also, the laws that Marx had created were, even in Gramsci's time, three quarters of a century old; *"How is it possible to consider the present, and quite specific present, with a mode of thought elaborated for a past which is often remote and superseded?"*[1] Finally, there was the blunt fact of failure; what the laws had predicted had not come to pass; the revolution that *had* occurred was in total contradiction of the laws. And apart from being incorrect, they were also dangerous, due to the lack of initiative that stemmed from popular belief in the laws.

Gramsci also dismissed the principle of centralisation, which he referred to as the 'Jacobin' model, although it was originally part of Marx's schema. This implies that he would have also excluded the command economy; and there is additional support for this in the fact that although he suggested a national co-ordination for the factory councils, the councils were to remain the primary decision-making centres.

Thus, Gramsci had in effect relegated virtually the whole of Marx's strategy, and much of Lenin's, to being no more than an outmoded footnote of history. He had created new plans and new policies, more practical and thought-out than

1. Antonio Gramsci *Prison Notebooks*, Lawrence and Wishart.

those of Marx, and considerably less authoritarian than those of Lenin. What he did not do was to supply a new scientific foundation for Marxism.

Although his proposed method of change had greater plausibility and appeal, it had less backing in terms of hard evidence. Gramsci offered no scientific laws, no precedents, no existing examples of workers councils taking control, no analysis of the practical obstructions, and no attempt to logically relate the causal relationships that might aid or hinder the progress of the socialist transformation.

In the total absence of any supporting evidence, whether logical or factual, one can only say that Gramsci's ideas are attractive; implausible, unrealistic, impractical, and utterly incapable of being initiated—but attractive. Which puts Gramsci's proposals on roughly the same footing as Erewhon, Utopia, or next year's Conservative Party manifesto. They are interesting to read or discuss, but absolutely useless as a plan to improve society.

But suppose Gramsci's scheme was practical, that there was perhaps some way of modifying his theories to make them usable; what would society be like after his trans-formations had occurred? It is not clear what type of government would exist because, while there would be a national co-ordinating group for the workers' councils, there would not be a communist party. Gramsci specifies that *"the party which proposes to put an end to class divisions will only achieve complete fulfilment when it ceases to exist because classes, and therefore their expressions, no longer exist"*.[1]

The prospect that this conjures up is uncertain to say the least. If there is no communist party, then surely there cannot be a communist government. What Gramsci presumably envisaged was that government as such would

1. Antonio Gramsci, op. cit.

cease to exist, and its various roles would be taken over locally by the factory councils, while national policy would be handled by the co-ordinating group. Such a system would be a little unwieldy, but at least it does not have the authoritarianism of Lenin's goal.

And what would their way of life by like? The Gramscian concept of ideological hegemony implies a culture biased and distorted by the presence of capitalism. The church is just another source of oppression, but on the other hand, it is the major foundation of the distorted moral values. With moral and material values corrupted by the establishment, it follows that all aspects of capitalist culture are spurious and false. After the initial period of instability, the whole ethos would be replaced by the new socialist integrated culture.

For a time, Gramsci supported the work of the Futurists, a movement whose paintings and sculpture tried to convey the energy of the new age, the machine age. The PSI ignored Futurism as it lacked a specific socialist content, something which did not concern Gramsci; it was enough for him that Futurism was an attack on the established values, the established forms of art. Although they were not political at that time, if they had been radicalised by the PSI, the Futurists could have become the basis for the new integrated culture. They would have provided the artistic content, while Gramsci and the PSI provided the moral and political values.

But if there are no scientific underpinnings to the political system one proposes, how can one say that the resultant culture is in any way superior to the preceding one? Stripped of the terminology, Gramsci was just comparing one ethos with another, and saying that the version he had put forward was better. Artistic values are often a matter of opinion, but the validity of the new society's moral values are of vital importance. And as Gramsci wrote very little about the specific faults of capitalism, or the detailed remedies to be offered by communism, it is impossible to say exactly what sort of morals were being suggested.

There is no doubt that Gramsci himself had high moral values, but it is essential to establish that the social organisation that he proposed would sustain those values. And if the intended society is neither inherently moral, nor scientifically valid, then it has very little to recommend it.

And what about the culture in the artistic sense? Art may be a matter of opinion, but it is an incredibly broad range of opinion. Gramsci was looking forward to a society where all art would be socialist art, would express socialist values, or would describe socialist beliefs. But despite the fairly broad range of subjects covered by communist theory, it is almost nothing compared with that covered by the arts.

Also, the Gramscian integrated culture implies an art that supports and propagandises the values of socialism; an art that not only restricts itself to good, socialist subjects, but that in any discussion automatically supports the party line. There shall be a socialist content to all art-forms, and yea, the word shall be shown as right, and righteous. This not only excludes all anti-socialist or pro-capitalist works, it also excludes forms of art that are totally neutral, completely lacking in political content. For if a work is not even concerned with politics, then it cannot have a socialist content.

An artistic environment of this sort can only be sterile and artificial, because in excluding non-political subjects, it also eliminates the subjects that have inspired the greatest works of art—love, truth, beauty, nature, and so on. Shakespeare's *Romeo and Juliet* was a study of how family relationships interfere with romantic relationships; Constable's primary concern was to depict the beauty of the countryside; Turner's interest was the interplay of light and shadow in sunlight; the sculpture of Naum Gabo is devoted to studying the boundaries between space and solid objects.

There are few, if any, great works of art that have an

explicitly political content, and to attempt to impose inappropriate limitations on art will only result in its becoming sterile, unappealing propaganda. To condemn politically neutral art as bourgeois rubbish—as has been said of Constable's work—is pathetic. It also shows total failure to understand what art or life are all about. All artists, from film-makers to poets, must be free to explore and interpret the world about them, to see and understand it in their own way, free from constraint or restrictions. This is equally true of people in general; the only difference is in the way the understanding is expressed.

Thus, Gramsci's greatest contribution to Marxism was to recognise that Marx's laws are neither scientific nor valid. In the place of historic inevitability, Gramsci proposes voluntarist change, propelled by the will and awareness of the people, and the efforts of the factory councils. But his method of change is actually impractical, while his ethos is no better, scientifically or morally, than the capitalist ethos it is supposed to replace. Indeed, the society it would create is an utterly repellent one.

But the existence of Gramsci's work does raise the possibility that as Marxism progresses, it will gradually come to reject the rules laid down by Marx. For example, Baran and Sweezy have written a Marxist critique of monopoly capitalism that completely ignores the concept of surplus value. Perhaps the Marxism of the future will be no more than a set of ideals; or perhaps it will stick to its outmoded laws, and become just another dogma.

8

Reasons to be Marxist

Why Choose Communism?

Most Marxists would probably claim that they follow
Marxism because it presents an accurate view of the world
and its faults, and how to change them. In other words, their
belief has a purely rational basis, founded on evidence. But
as has been shown, the theories of Marxism are outdated and
irrelevant, the 'scientific' method is illogical, the
transitional phase is unnecessary, potentially dangerous,
but is not transitory, while the higher phase is only vaguely
described, and inconsistent. An economy based on Marxist
principles is unworkable, and Marxist countries are
successful only according to the degree that these principles
are eliminated from the economy.

In fact, there is very little good at all to be said about
communism in practice; except that in some ways it is better
than capitalism. Apart from being a merely relative
superiority, not an absolute one, it is also a selective claim;
communists are obliged to narrow their field of vision
considerably to see only the evidence which shows
capitalism as the inferior system. And if their belief is not
purely rational, then there must be other, non-rational
reasons why they adhere to Marxism.

It is important to analyse and understand these motives
because they give a guide as to how individuals will act in

real-life situations. Their stated ideals may be liberal, but the ideology itself can operate in extremely authoritarian ways, and it is essential to know if the people we are dealing with are liberals—as they claim—or merely power-seekers. When the stated principles conflict with personal goals, it is inevitable that the principles will be discarded.

Another point is that a person's motives are often less coherently analysed than their factual belief system; motives are rooted in the emotions rather rational analysis. So a person may have misguided motives, leading them to believe in a misguided theory.

One of the major advantages that Marxism has is that it is an old and established theory. The 130 years that have passed since Marx wrote the Manifesto have given communists plenty of time to build up an international organisation, the roots of which existed prior to Marx's joining the Communist League. The passing of time not only assists recruitment—it also gives respect and credibility; people think that anything that has been around for that long must be valid. The assumption is that if the system was irrational it would have been disproved and discarded by now—it has not been discarded, therefore it cannot be irrational, so it must be valid.

But it is precisely because it is not rational that Marxism is able to survive attempts at disproof. As was shown earlier, it is not a falsifiable theory, and can ride over any apparent errors with claims that the dialectical process has been at work, or that communism must of necessity be a global system, or even offer cliches like 'the chain breaks at its weakest link'. Its survival has not been due to its rationality, but to its carefully applied irrationality—which continues to be tolerated and accepted by all its followers.

Knowledge progresses as time passes, and what was considered a fact a hundred years ago, turns out to be just another strange theory. But sometimes theories have lives beyond any rational justification—the idea that God created the world, or that the earth is flat—or the theories of Marx. A hundred years ago British capitalism was utterly exploitative, virtually without any redeeming features, and Marx's unqualified criticism of it was justified, as was his willingness to accept anything other than the then existing system. But the world has changed; capitalism is no longer a totally malignant system, but Marxists still hold that nineteenth century vision.

The age of Marxism is not an indication of its respectability, but a sign that it is time for new theories. And its continued survival is not a proof of its validity, but merely a result of its ability to evade disproof.

The reasons behind the continuing popularity of communism can probably be found in the psychological factors that cause people to want to believe in it. One of the most common of these is the element of revenge; capitalists will not merely be removed by the proposed society—they will be 'got'—they will be punished. This attitude comes out in private discussions rather than in Marxist texts, but it is clear that many Marxists, if not actually motivated by anger or revenge, at least feel it, and regard it as justification for their aims. It is an entirely understandable attitude, and many of the schemes carried out by some companies certainly deserve some form of punishment. But there is a danger that the justification of anger or of the desire for revenge will be so satisfying to Marxists that they do not seek a detailed analysis of society's faults, or a rational method of correcting those faults.

They will be unquestioningly tolerant of the aims of communism, or the practicality of those aims, because anything which removes the capitalists from power will be seen as automatically beneficial. Never mind the fact that a revolution may not create a utopia—it *will* get rid of the establishment. Or in the context of contemporary politics, never mind the fact that nationalisation is, almost without exception, an economic failure, it will remove the capitalists from the positions of wealth.

A related source of popular appeal is the fact that communism claims an inherent moral superiority. Capitalism is based on selfishness and greed, while communism is based on equality and cooperation, so it is automatically the better of the two. But pure theory does not, and cannot have, inherent moral superiority. It may express great ideals, it may speak of only the most altruistic goals, its creator may have high moral standards, and he may explain his views in his writings. But the practical application of his theory may be utterly different from what he envisages on paper. And a theory cannot justifiably claim any greater moral value than that existing in its actual operation.

The proposals put forward by communism are so vague as to allow an extremely broad range of systems to exist, all operating within the loosely defined parameters of Marxism, and all presumably have an equal right to describe themselves as morally valid forms. And this is nonsense; a repressive, authoritarian system can never be morally justified; and if one of the resultant systems is immoral, the best that can be said about its originating theory is that it is amoral; it is without morals, even unrelated to morality. The theory does not define a specific society with given moral characteristics; it merely offers certain vague generalisations which could apply to almost any type of society.

Nonetheless, the moral stance of some Marxists is extremely strident, even verging on hysterical. Capitalism is not merely harmful, it is positively evil; this is considered to be true of every type of capitalism, and of everything touched by it. It distorts society, economic truth, and even the principles on which science is based, as the perversion of economic science spills over to corrupt all fields of knowledge. Hoffman, when describing the dubious psychology which attempts to prove that some races are genetically inferior to others, refers to the *"empiricist lie"*[1] that a difference in behaviour is proof of inferiority. In Hoffman's eyes, even facts are lies; the very basis of science is false.

What Hoffman should have been attacking is not the empirical data, but the interpretations made from that data; facts are facts, but deducing a relationship between the facts can be wide open to the scientist's imagination. Perhaps racist psychology is above questions of morality—it is either good science or bad science, justified or unjustified interpretations of the facts.

The attempt to replace bourgeois morality with Marxist morality is futile. It would be useless for any organisation— political, economic, or religious—to claim that its particular brand of morality was the right, and only acceptable type of morality. There are no brands or 'isms' in ethics; there is only right and wrong. If for example, leaders of business happened to claim that their wages policies, which cause low incomes, poverty, and exploitation, were justified and morally acceptable, it would not be necessary to invoke a new brand of morality to dispute the claim. Exploitation is wrong, no matter how carefully worded the justification is, and regardless of how loudly it is publicised. The logic of the claim is false, and the ability to promote it so widely is offensive; but this does indicate any need for a new brand of ethics; what is needed is greater study of the policies and effects of capitalism.

But morality should not be sought in a political ideology or organisation—it should be sought in ways of living that operate in an effectively ethical manner. Ideally, people should seek morality within themselves, working out their own rules, their own ethics, living to the highest standards

1. John Hoffman *Marxism and the Theory of Praxis.*

they can set themselves, and making sure that none of their actions have any harmful effects on others. They should not be bound by the rigid rules of some century old, or even two thousand year old system that has answers for everything, but lacks the flexibility to allow the individual to find his own answers.

The blanket condemnation of capitalism and its related ethics tend to discourage thought or rational analysis. It is not a question for study or future consideration, it is an axiom, a closed issue, a basic principle that must be accepted in order to allow adherents to move on to the next question. It is not a matter of calmly studying capitalism to see which aspects are beneficial, which aspects are harmful, and to what degree; instead, the entire system is mentally consigned to the scrapheap. And that is an excellent way to create blind, unthinking followers, with the unavoidable corollary, followers who lack any real understanding of what they are condemning or why.

In such a context, it ceases to be a question of morality—it is just another item of party policy, established dogma. The person who follows the party line is neither thinking or acting in a moral way, he is merely obeying the rules. Moral behaviour must involve choice and understanding, and when both of these are absent, we cannot say of an individual that he is acting on high moral values; after all, he is only obeying orders. Such a policy might, in the short term, ensure that the organisation's behaviour adheres to a rigid moral code, but in the long term, as the followers of yesterday become the leaders of today, the organisation will become bogged down in an inability to understand real moral issues.

Related to the high moral tone is the fact that communism is also a cause, a noble ideal. It may have faults in theory, or even in practice sometimes, but is principles are aimed at creating a better world. Marxists want to abolish poverty, inequality, injustice, oppression, and exploitation. Communism offers a better life, and the offer of such a life, even just the offer of the goal of the ideal, is more than enough to overcome any aversion to the faults that occur in practice. Utopia, peace, and human harmony are all inspiring goals, and compared to the failings of capitalism, the principles of communism generate automatic sympathy.

Capitalism—to its critics in the western, industrialised nations—represents the mundane, ugly and brutal real world. In a way its faults are seen as the natural faults of reality—unavoidable but unattractive. The ideal of communism is, quite reasonably, more attractive; and made ten times more so by the fact that it is just an ideal. To some it may seem unattainable; which means it is a cause they can safely devote their entire lives to, and never lose that ideal. But in terms of changing society, of eliminating the evils of capitalism, it is a dedication that is completely wasted.

But there is a danger that in attempting to attack every unpleasant aspect of society as a direct fault of capitalism that a good deal of accuracy is lost in the process. The argument is, capitalism is bad, therefore everything related to it, or stemming from it is also bad. With such reasoning, it is obvious that one must both ignore contrary evidence, and claim the existence of supporting evidence. Where no support exists, it is enough to merely imply the existence of a causal relationship. For example, Hoffman, in attaking racist psychology, implies that capitalism has corrupted the very foundations of science.

Nothing escapes criticism. Some Marxists, seeing the failure of democracy to cater for the needs of minorities, attack democracy itself, instead of trying to locate specific faults, and re-structure society into a more welfare orientated system. Inflation and unemployment are not regarded as accidental failings in a complex economy, but as deliberate policies, consciously designed to reduce the standard of living of the working man.

Marxism claims to explain everything—class conflict, history, racism in psychology, inflation, unemployment, depression, poverty, imperialism, crime, and war, are all covered by one Marxist tract or another. This is partly because there are so many variations of Marxism; reformist and revolutionary, followers of the young Marx or the mature Marx, those who have revised his theories and those who still adhere to the original principles, and finally, those who have moved on to newer teachers, such as Lenin and Mao. Within this range there is a wealth of scope for anyone seeking answers to the problems of society.

And this is yet another source of the continued popularity of Marxism; something for everyone. For almost anyone who opposes the existing system, there is a brand of communist philosophy that is just right for them. It is an off-the-peg philosophy; decide what you want, and make your choice. Choose between the liberalism of the young, idealistic Marx, or the autoritarianism of Stalin; between the scientific determinism of the mature Marx, or the personally-controlled destiny of Gramsci.

But in being all things for all men, what it gains in popularity, it loses in validity. It is not possible for all the various forms of Marxism to be the right way, there cannot be a dozen different answers as to how society should be changed. Only one of them can be correct—at the very maximum. But all the indications are that none of them is correct.

In attempting to prove the accuracy of their theories, facts are distorted in a way that would not be acceptable in any real science. For example, I have been told that inflation is the balancing factor in the capitalist equation; apparently there is a mathematical equation somewhere which defines the capitalist system in its entirety, but to make it balance, there must be inflation. The discovery that inflation now exists in Russia is glossed over with claims that the close inter-relationship between the Soviet economy and the western capitalist countries has had an unavoidable effect on Russia, and that it is 'importing' inflation. Presumably the western nations are also 'importing' inflation, but to a much higher degree, owing to the higher levels of trade.

Marxists wish to show that communism has none of the problems of capitalism; theirs is a totally different system, without any faults whatsoever. To make such a claim is very easy, in fact, easier said than done. And when it becomes obvious that the claim was false, then the public relations men appear with glib explanations. But nothing has been learnt, nothing proved; there is as much substance in their predictions as there is in a politician's promises.

But despite all the other factors, the age of communism, its moral superiority, and its claims to explain almost everything, perhaps the most important reason for its continued support is the fact that, throughout its lifespan, it has been the only alternative to capitalism. Anyone who disagreed with the existing system had only one opposition group to turn to, only one possible alternate ideology. This meant that communism attracted followers simply because the existing form of capitalism had faults. There was a simple choice between one or the other ideology—or an intellectual wasteland with no coherent views, no attempts at explanation, no moral basis, no unifying theory, and no practical programme.

There have been attempts to modify capitalism, for example, the co-operative movement, the Social Credit theories, but these usually revolved around one or two minor changes, with no cohesive view of the economy in general. And there is no point in suggesting any sort of change to the economy, major or minor, unless one can show how that change will affect the rest of the economy. To do this, one needs a coherent theory, an understanding of how society operates, and an awareness of the need for real change.

But the ideas put forward were usually just tinkering with

the system, rather than seeking to transform it. The nearest there has been to a successful modification of capitalism is the worker participation system in Germany; but this has not changed society, or the structure of the economy. The need for a total metamorphosis is so obvious to most people, that a mere tinkering is not worth considering; it fails to take account of what is needed, therefore, it cannot offer what is needed.

So the opponent of capitalism turned automatically to communism; an imperfect system, but one with ample scope for a personal choice of what seemed the most accurate and practical explanation. And despite the hardening of its intellectual arteries, there was still some room for new ideas, new developments.

There was a broad range to choose from, but beneath that umbrella, it was the only choice, the only alternative. Until now. There is now another theory, opposed to the poverty and exploitation which continue under the existing form of capitalism, and opposed also to the authoritarian nature of communism. The last chapter of this book will try to explain some of the reasoning behind the new system, while the next chapter will be devoted to analysing some of the requirements of a genuinely beneficial social structure.

9

Free Selections

The Need for Freedom of Choice

The primary claim of communism is that it offers equality, and social welfare for all. Throughout communist literature the emphasis is on the community, the mass of the people, the collectivity; the whole population is cared for, as a group. Capitalism on the other hand, maximises welfare by mass production, with the emphasis on the individual, who makes personal decisions as to what to buy, where to work, and where to live. In theory there should be no difference between the two. One promises to look after the whole community, and by doing so must presumably look after each and every individual; the other system concerns itself with the individual, but by doing so, must surely be guaranteeing the well-being of all. In theory . . .

In practice, things are different. Under communism, everyone owns the factors of production—on paper; but only a tiny minority have the power to control, to decide methods of production, what shall be produced, and at what price it will be sold. With capitalism, the right to own and control is theoretically universal, but in reality is limited to a very few; in most western industrialised nations we do not have capitalism in its pure form, but monopoly capitalism, which is something else.

There are many ways in which one could categorise the failings of each system, but in the most basic terms, the common factor is the absence of choice. Each ideology makes for, or imposes on the citizen, a number of pre-decided choices, thus limiting the choices that the individual can make for himself. Each of these doctrines offers things, objects, material welfare, but neither offers all its people the right to choose their own way of life, and this is the crucial fault in both systems. The concentration of power in the hands of the state or the monopolies is no more than the means by which this restriction is achieved; the real fault is the denial of the right to choose.

The ideal system would be one which maximised the range of choice open to people, and although it is obvious that no society will ever be able to offer total, unlimited choice, it is clear that the existing alternatives are grossly unsatisfactory. Choice must be limited by purely practical considerations of what is actually possible, and by moral considerations of what can be done without harming others. But these are merely the obvious and basic reservations; beyond these, there should be no external, imposed restrictions whatsoever.

The roots of freedom must go back to education, because many of our choices are limited by what we have been taught is possible. And it seems undeniable that, in this country at least, most people are taught to think of themselves as potential employees. At school we are taught to consider our future job opportunities, our need for qualifications, and our need to have skills that are useful to employers—to convince the employer that we are worth taking on. Children are not taught to develop their skills as an end in itself; they are not given an understanding of society that could help them make objective judgements of it; they are not encouraged to develop their abilities according to their own goals in life.

In all these ways our choices are being limited; not by any legislative or financial barriers, but through the way in which we are encouraged to look at things. We are persuaded to see our working life as employment, and our goal in respect of that life is to obtain the best possible type of employment; because life depends on the maximum level of material well-being.

So the first thing we need to create complete freedom is a very simple, but monumental change; a change in attitudes. We must educate children for their own benefit, not turn them into factory fodder. They must be allowed to develop their full potential, to study any and every subject that they wish to learn about. They should be taught everything they need, and everything they want; education should be used to expand their horizons, not limit them.

A person's way of life should be entirely his or her own choice, and should not be interfered with in any way whatsoever. This means not only the right to choose, but also the right to know wht the alternatives are, and the availability of all the alternatives. If people are entitled to freedom of choice, they are entitled to all the corollaries that are necessary to provide a genuine and meaningful freedom. They should not only have all the information they need, they should be free from inaccurate and biased information.

Leaving aside future changes in education, we can now consider the general requirements and benefits of free choice. A good education should include coverage of the various economic ideologies, philosophies, and differing ways of life, to allow each person to choose from the different life-styles. Such information would include details of the benefits of property ownership versus renting, employment vs. company formation, materialism vs. asceticism, and so on. Equipped with such details, citizens could make much more personally useful decisions.

But one cannot equip a person for their entire life; circumstances change, and what is true one year may not be true the next year. Taxes, wages, rents, etc. all vary, therefore the relative merits of any particular course will also change. What is far more important than learning a set of rules is that people should learn how to learn; this applies to all fields of knowledge, but in the case that we are studying it is necessary so that people can adapt to alterations in circumstances. They must know the rules and relationships that apply at the time, and they must also be aware that rules fluctuate. So when changes do occur, they can decide whether or not they can, or wish to, adapt to them.

But although one can give information to people, and teach them that some aspects of it may vary, one cannot force them to learn, or to understand, or to utilise the knowledge they have. People often do not realise the importance of analysing their decisions, or of taking control of the events which influence their lives. Sometimes they seem unaware of the effect their decisions could have, and sometimes they seem not to care. They pay whatever sum of income tax the Inland Revenue asks for, without even attempting to get all their allowances included. They buy whatever car or television takes their fancy, without any analysis of which one is the best value for money, or has the lowest running costs, or the greatest reliable life-span. And very often they make what a prudent observer might call a 'wrong' decision. The person may be quite happy with their choice, but in the long term, a series of such decisions can be expensive.

Yet if people have a right to free choice, they also have a right to misuse that choice. The government, or the prudent observer, or the Consumers' Association, may say that a particular decision was not the best possible one—in purely objective terms—but they do not have a right to force people to make 'good' decisions; nor should they have such a right. Every person should be allowed to make wrong decisions in every aspect of their lives, from drinking and smoking, to overpaying income tax, to choosing poor bargains in consumer goods.

This is not to say that we should not care if people make mistakes, but that beyond a certain point we do not have the right to interfere. If people are to have genuine free choice, we cannot give it to them with one hand, and then legislate some options out of existence. To take control of people's lives in this way is not only arrogant, it is also short-sighted. The experience of life itself is one of the best teachers that anyone could have, and to insulate people from the effects of their wrong decisions is to insulate them from life; to separate them from their own lives.

In thinking about the results of faulty decisions the person eventually comes to a much better understanding of why their selection was wrong. Perhaps it would have been possible for some teacher to say, 'Never spend money on clothes unnecessarily, never buy cars that are not worth the money'. But such statements are too vague to be meaningful; and even precisely phrased statements would still not have the impact that knowledge gained from personal experience has. To learn from experience is to learn where the borderlines are, where black or white fade into gray uncertainty, and further study is required. It is to learn what wrong decisions mean personally, how serious the effect can be, and how vulnerable one is to particular types of error.

One also learns to distinguish those choices which may seem obviously wrong, but are personally right. For example, some people might actually prefer to spend money on frivolous clothes, or an unreliable car. The purely subjective pleasure gained from certain types of clothing, or certain makes of car, may outweigh the financial costs, thus making what seems to be an error into a simple value judgement.

So if the individual has been allowed to make wrong decisions, and not swamped by an over-protective welfare state, or starved of choice by an inefficient centralised state, he or she can make a multitude of errors. And each fault can lead to learning and understanding, to a greater awareness of the borderline uncertainties of life, and even to a greater knowledge of one's own personal preferences.

Thus, the availability of free choice is not only essential to the consumer to allow him to assess the merits and subjective benefits of the various goods; it is also of enormous advantage in terms of personal development. This process which so aids the consumer is also one of the forces that assists the effectiveness of competition. In deciding which goods to make, or stock, or how to price them, the seller is also liable to make errors, and in doing so leaves himself vulnerable to the consequences of his actions.

Each wrong decision that the seller makes loses sales or profits for him; if he prices his goods too highly, his customers will go elsewhere; if his prices are too low, then his sales income will not be enough to keep him in business. This is why competition is sometimes described as an information mechanism; even when the seller has no idea of the prices asked by other dealers, he cannot help but be aware of the results. He learns whether or not he is pricing his goods correctly by whether or not he earns enough money to stay in business. And if he doesn't learn, then his income falls, and he does indeed go out of business.

The monopoly company is insulated from this learning mechanism; if its prices are too high, people will still buy its goods, because as consumers they have no choice. It is rare for a company to dominate an entire market, but even in a normal situation with just a few companies in control, an oligopoly market, the corporation has sufficient power for effective control. It shares its market with one or two other corporations with similar attitudes, and does not need to actually compete for custom. It does not have to lower its prices, or maintain its quality standards, or make any special effort to attract customers. It is selling a product that people have to buy, and if they wish to buy it, they must do so on the monopoly's conditions.

So if prices are too high, or for the sake of argument, too low, the monopoly remains invulnerable to harm. And being unable to suffer harm, there is nothing to encourage it to re-examine its policies; there is no learning process. The monopoly cannot be persuaded by rational discussion to examine its actions, for in its own terms it is not doing anything wrong. It is making or selling, and the customers are buying; and of course, profits are good. This is the eternal guideline for every big corporation; if profits are high, then lots of people must be buying the product, and if they are buying, then they must be happy with it.

For the corporation to admit otherwise would be to admit the existence of monopoly power—and would cast doubt on its value to society. And real-world companies have to worry about public relations, and the corporate image. The theoretical big company of economics is somewhat different; it does not have to worry about public relations, it is free from all the taints and miscalculations of human nature; it is perfect, and perfectly efficient.

The centralised economy is exactly the same; it is perfectly efficient, rational, carefully planned, and the ideal system— on paper. In practice it is unwieldy, and offers little or no choice to the consumer; what choice it does give is between inferior goods, unsuitable ones, or nothing at all. No state organisation can ever be vulnerable to mere market forces, unless the state wishes it to be so. And if they are not subject to harm, there is no information mechanism; there is nothing to show the managers or the policy makers that they have made faulty decisions regarding product design, production methods, quality control, and so on. So they carry on turning out tractors with missing batteries, shoes that fall apart, and all the other disasters of an unplanned economy.

So for most people, choice is not a very real thing, regardless of the system they live under. What is needed is an economic structure that does offer choice—in every sense of the word, in every aspect of life. For a start, such a system must offer a wide and varied range of goods, from a large number of independent producers, each one trying as hard as possible to make what people want at a price they are willing to pay. These firms must be independent of one another, or of any external agency, but must still be dependent on the consumer's good will. They must seek to, and need to, provide the products that people want.

There must also be financial equality, indeed, this is a primary requirement for any system that claims to offer social justice, for without equality there can be no real justice. This is not to say there must be absolute equality, with everybody earning exactly the same wage, or as in Marx's proposal, with wages being carefully balanced to allow for each individual's family needs. Neither total uniformity nor planned inequality are acceptable, as both would limit the individual's choice; they would be oppressive, yet not be the most beneficial way.

Some people do not want or need large sums of money; their needs are emotional rather than financial; or they may have inexpensive requirements instead of costly ones. On the other hand, there are people who give preference to material goods over emotional needs. A society of genuine free choice should be able to allow both types of person to have what they want. This means that the people themselves should be able to set their income level—not the government, nor the state companies, nor the big monopolies, but the individuals themselves.

What is wrong with the existing structures is not that there *is* inequality, but that the inequality is so great that some people have virtually unlimited resources, while others do not even have enough for the basic necessities of life. And society is structured so that at the lower end of the income scale, not only do the victims suffer from extremely unpleasant living conditions, but they are trapped in those conditions.

There are some rare types—monks, recluses—who would be quite happy with low wages, and would not want any sort of luxury in their surroundings. They might even seek this as a way of life, and not regard themselves as at all deprived. But the essential feature is the element of choice; the inhabitants of big-city slums have not chosen to take low wages, nor have they sought to live in slums. Both have been forced upon them by society.

It would appear that there is no great degree of poverty under communism, that is, considering the level of economic development of most communist countries. Instead, there is a social structure that cannot be changed by any means at all, regardless of the number of people who want it to change. There are extensive infringements of civil liberties, ranging from police harassment of minor dissidents, to a virtual ban on genuine trade unions, to imprisonment or labour camps for the more outspoken dissidents.

Thus, there is no opportunity for any individual—or indeed, any number of individuals, even 90% of the population—to alter any part of the political, social, or economic structure of such a country. This accusation is aimed primarily at the Eastern Bloc nations, but remains valid as a possible path for future developments for any communist country. And in these countries, not only is it impossible to change the system, it is illegal to want to change it; to say that the country is mismanaged is a criminal offence.

So there is no freedom of choice about the type of society one lives in, no choice about one's personal way of life, and not even the right to think for oneself.

These rights must surely be the most basic of all, yet in many communist countries they are flatly denied. A doctrine which places unlimited power in the hands of the ruling class, and no countervailing power in the hands of the people, should create no surprises when the power is abused. The fact that the results are the total opposite of the goals that Marx expressed is only a passing irony; or further proof of the falsity of his theories. The revolution is aimed at abolishing all classes, but succeeds only in simplifying down to two classes—the controllers and the workers. The aim was to abolish the ownership of property; it does this by universalising theoretical ownership, and centralising the real control, the actual basis of class power.

But there are two aspects of class; control of the factors of production is only one: the other aspect is the ability to transmit or acquire control. In most capitalist countries a major proportion of the rich have obtained their wealth by an accident of birth; they have become wealthy because of who they were born to, rather than any conscious effort to seek affluence. And the few people who are able to acquire riches independently are also able to pass on their acquisitions to their children, thus perpetuating the family basis of the wealth. And this is the aspect of class which is central to the present discussion.

In the same way that the rich are placed and maintained in their positions by birth, so are the poor; but unfortunately for them, they are in a considerably less attractive position. The child born to a poor family starts off with sub-standard hospital facilities, creating a dramatic difference in infant mortality figures between the top income group and the lowest income group. General health care is also inferior, and this, combined with the fact that very poor families are usually forced to live in slums, means that the child's health suffers.

Slum areas often have sub-standard schools as well, so the child goes from an overcrowded, badly-built home, to an overcrowded, run-down school, which has out of date text-books, inadequate heating, small classrooms, and a shortage of equipment. The child gets little encouragement to study at home, and indeed, would find it hard to do so anyhow. And the school, instead of compensating for the home disadvantages, merely exacerbates them. Because of the poverty at home, the child is forced to leave school earlier than his middle class counterpart, to get a job and add to the family income. But in leaving earlier, he leaves with less qualifications, and so is not able to get such a good job; that is, he must accept one with a lower income or poorer prospects.

Thus, the cycle of poverty continues, and the existence of low income becomes the creation of a class structure. The child's position in life is fixed from the moment of birth. There is no free choice at all; merely a slight chance that the very determined will succeed in some way.

The only differences are that under capitalism, the disadvantaged are condemned to poverty, while under communism they are forced into a life that has been pre-chosen, and controlled by, the state. They are totally dependent on the state for their education, health care, housing, and employment. This direction of dependency is the absolute reverse of what it should be; the state should have to rely on the people. The state should not be able to exist without the support of the people, as it is nothing more than an artificial mechanism created to benefit its citizens.

The citizen cannot be independent of the state unless he can be financially independent; everything revolves around this, just as in Marx's scheme where the worker is forced to sell his labour to the capitalist to survive. Having no capital of his own, he is obliged to accept whatever wages are offered because he lacks bargaining power; similarly, under comunism he is forced to accept whatever conditions are offered because he lacks bargaining power. By banning privately owned businesses, or by limiting the size allowed to the very smallest, least efficient, most vulnerable level, the state eliminates the threat of any citizen ever having the strength to argue with the state.

Even if there was no possibility of communism deteriorating into totalitarianism, and it was proved to be a beneficial system, there would still be no justification for imposing it on people. They have a right to live their own way of life, and a right to change the existing structure of society; the right to freedom of choice in the widest possible sense.

This means creating a society that cares for its people, but does not control them. Where people can seek their own way of life, without exploiting or being exploited. Such a system requires a very specific form of economic structure, one that is not provided by either monopoly capitalism, or communism. The next chapter will argue, from Marx's own goals, what that structure should be.

10

Back to Square One

Marxist Ideals – But a Different Policy

By now, we can discard Marx's prescriptions for curing the ills of society, having shown them to be outdated, impractical, and potentially dangerous. Yet we are still left with the question, surely the body politic suffers from some undeniably serious ailments, and if Marx's cure was wrong, what can be done?

Society is indeed sick, and Marx himself might have seen the correct answer if only he had examined his thoughts a little more carefully. Indeed, the solution to the problem can be deduced from Marx's own words. Perhaps if he had been a little more open-minded in his approach, or used greater scientific care in his analysis, he would have seen some of the implications of his own statements. But Marx's background was philosophy, and contorted nineteenth century philosophy at that, rather than analytic science. It is also clear that Marx had already made up his mind regarding solutions by the time that he and Engels wrote the Manifesto, and *The German Ideology*.

Years later, in preparing to write *Capital*, he accumulated vast amounts of research; but no new learning, or under-standing, or opinions on society are detectable. Marx spent most of *Capital* attacking the conditions that the workers and the poor suffered; but he was not able to see how those conditions were changing. Nor did he analyse cures in detail, but merely repeated, or referred to, the same sort of vague statements he had made elsewhere.

Without wishing to imply that the following sections represent a Marxist analysis, it is still worth considering Marx's own words, to see what sort of system they could refer to. A society based on Marx's timeless ideals, but separated from his outdated goals.

Marx's main objection was to the exploitation of the workers, which the capitalists were able to continue because they owned the factoriers, and the workers owned nothing. The workers had no choice except poverty—which in many eras was virtually a punishable offence—or exploitation. It is this enormous gap between owning and not owning that is the central theme of his work. But that gap becomes a chasm when one considers the scale of the businesses that the capitalists had.

Marx makes a number of references to the unpleasant effects of monopoly, and it is clear throughout his writings that his primary target is the monopolist or large-scale industry, operating as they do at a level which utterly dwarfs the worker. But it is rare for him to actually state that it is big business he is attacking: rare, but not unknown. *"Big industry makes for the worker not only the relation to the capitalist, but labour itself, unbearable."*[1]

Big business has greater wealth and power than even the most affluent capitalist mill-owner, and therefore has a greater ability to exploit. It represented a major step along the path of accumulation that Marx had described; increasing concentration of capital in few and few companies, and an ever-smaller number of capitalists. Eventually there might be just one company in each industry —or perhaps just *one* company—the final monopoly. And then there would be no limit to the exploitation that could be

1. Marx and Engels *The German Ideology*, Lawrence and Wishart.

achieved.

Marx was repelled by the vision of a handful of companies, or men, dominating the economy, and in its place he sought to replace *"the domination of circumstances and of chance over individuals by the domination of individuals over chance and circumstances"*.[1] Men should control their own lives, not be controlled by big business. To achieve this, the *"mass of instruments of production must be made subject to each individual, and property to all. Modern universal intercourse can be controlled by individuals, therefore, only when controlled by all"*.[2]

But as has been shown, an economy in which everything is theoretically owned by all, while controlled by a few, simply becomes authoritarian. And in Yugoslavia, where the factories are owned by all, and genuinely run by the majority of the workers, it is unwieldy and clumsy. Some other method of allocating ownership and management functions is necessary, so that power is decentralised, equality is encouraged, and management is efficient.

One possible course would be to have the factors of production divided up into small units, so that each person could own, *and control*, his private section of the economy. This is in fact, the only possible way for every individual to have complete control over the business that he works for; because any form of collective ownership or collective management must remove some fraction of control, either by state decree, or by the need to compromise, to adjust to the group consensus. No other form could exist which would give the individual such complete control over his 'employer'. Therefore, no other structure could exist which could increase the aggregate power of the citizens over the means of production.

1. Marx and Engels, op. cit.
2. Marx and Engels, op. cit.

This would be the direct opposite of the monopolies and joint stock companies that Marx condemned, and is perfectly in line with the ideals expressed in the preciding quotation; and the following one. *"The all-round development of the individual will only cease to be conceived as ideal, as vocation, etc. when the impact of the world which stimulates the real development of the abilities of the individual comes under the control of the individuals themselves, as the communists desire".* [1]

So perhaps the ideal form of communism is a totally fractionated economy; the extreme form of small business economy. Not exactly the path that Marx had envisioned, but then his path has been shown to be impassable. And there is one other problem; such a system is not practical.

For most types of business, especially in manufacturing, the one-man company is just too small to be efficient. A single individual just cannot have all the time, money, space, skills, and equipment necessary for say, an electro-plating works, or a building company. And in advanced industry, like petro-chemicals or mass-production, a one-man show is just out of the question.

So there is no practical method by which each and every worker can be given full control of the company he works for. But is this actually necessary? All that is really needed is that the company's policies take note of society's needs, treat the workers as human beings, treat the customers with respect, and that the worker—indeed any citizen—has full control over his or her life. None of these conditions automatically entail any institutionalised control over industry; if the structure of the economy, market forces, or the need to conform to accepted modes of behaviour are sufficient to achieve these conditions, then no further controls are required.

1. Marx and Engels, op. cit.

Thus, we need a structure in which companies do not have great power, where they cannot fix prices arbitrarily, and where they are dependent on the customer's good will. A society in which economic and political power are separate, and the state is controlled by the people, not by minority vested interests. An economy which is controlled by the largest number of people, preferably such a large number that they cannot form a closed, coherent social group. An economy in which those who do not control corporate policy abstain because they do not need, and do not want control. A society in which incomes are roughly equal, and each individual's income is determined by a personal decision, not by external forces.

The crucial factors are the individual's ability to run his life—or in Marx's terms, to dominate circumstance and chance; and a degree of control over corporate policies—the instruments of production being subject to all. These require that the organisations of society have a certain vulnerability to the members of society, that their strength, political or otherwise, be fairly evenly matched. The citizen should have the same power to fight the state or the corporations, as they have to attack the citizen.

To provide this, two basic conditions must be fulfilled—there must be a high level of financial equality, and the organisations of society must be of a scale that human beings can cope with. The first condition gives the individual the financial power to fight the system, or become totally independent of it; to save, to sue, or to create his own source of income. The second condition ensures that no organisation can ever have the power to place its values, opinions, or even its survival, above those of the people it is designed to serve. The type of organisation that this implies brings us to a society of small businesses and decentralised government.

It has been shown that the extreme form of small business economy is not practical, but with a slightly larger, more realistic scale of company, such an economy most definitely is feasible. Not companies with just one person—although that is an operatable size for some types of business—but companies with up to 500 workers. This might not seem very large, but to see such a company is to realise that it is a thriving concern, an efficient business, providing jobs, and capable of creating employment opportunities for the future. Such a company can often be very impressive in terms of sales.

For example, BCB Pipefreezing, with only 30 employees, has a turnover (1980) of £500,000. As anyone with a bank account will recognise, this is quite a lot of money. Prestwick Circuits, a printed circuit-board manufacturer with 175 employees, had a sales total (1979) of £6 million. This is a company that was able to invest £1,000,000 in new equipment in 1979, and is able to compete successfully in the world markets. A company with as many as 500 workers could have a turnover as high as £30 million, or even higher; yet by current U.K. standards it would be a small company.

If we take firms with 500 – 2,000 employees as medium size companies, and anything above that to be a big company, we find that the big business is truly beyond any human comprehension. Its size can be measured, its factories can be counted, the effects of its operations can be analysed; but it is impossible to appreciate emotionally, by direct experience, how vast such an enterprise is. It is a force that no individual could create or control, is often beyond even the power of governments, while nations themselves can be pawns to the great multinationals.

To give a numerical indicator of the size of one of them, Shell's profits in 1979 were £3.05 billion: their sales were £34.8 billion. Thus, Shell's sales were 68,000 times the size of BCB's, cited above, yet BCB is of a size that would represent the peak of ambition to some budding businessmen.

The big corporation has the power to defy governments, trade unions, consumers, or even the supposedly impregnable laws of the market. It can hold wages down during a boom, or keep profits and prices up during a recession. It represents the total negation of all market theory economics, while what it offers is simply a moderate version of the evils Marx described in *Capital*.

But none of this is true of the small company. A firm which supplies only 1% of its particular market cannot have great power over that market. A company with only 500 employees cannot demand government assistance if it is in danger of bankruptcy; it does not have the power to demand changes in corporate tax law, nor can it back up its demands with threats to leave the country. More importantly, a small business economy is one which is controlled by the greatest possible number of people, and so is as close as is practical to the ideal stated by Marx, that the economy should be controlled by all.

It must be admitted that the small firms in such an economy would not be controlled by all—at least, not directly; not that is, the direct domination that operates in Russia, or the universal access to management that exists in Yugoslavia. But as has been shown, it is not practical for everyone to have direct managerial control over all factors of the economy. Nonetheless, in its own way the small business economy is run by the people.

The fact that the small firm only provides a tiny proportion of the market that it operates in, means that it is genuinely in competition with other firms. It must persuade each and every customer that its products are better, or more suitable, or more attractive, than those of its competitors. Each sale lost is a cause for concern, and any swing of mood against the firm or its products could wipe it out of existence.

The small firm, unlike the big corporation, is subject to

the laws of the market. It cannot set its prices too high, sell inferior goods, or artificially control demand. It cannot impose its own wishes on the consumer— *"any colour, so long as its black"*, any beer so long as its gassy lager, or any bread so long as its tasteless, de-naturised sponge. The big company uses its advertising budget, and its total control over the sales outlets, to force people to buy what it wishes to sell. In the centralised economy, the state has total power over what is sold. But the small firm must sell what the market requires.

Yet 'the market' is merely a shorthand name for the accumulated decisions of all consumers, so to say that the small firm must follow the dictates of the market, is to say that it must obey the wishes of the people. It must sell what the people want, at a price, quality, and variety of choice that the people demand.

Thus, in a genuine free market economy, even though there may be no direct managerial, legislative, or state control over business, the very structure of the system gives the consumer—the citizen—total, indirect control over company policies.

This control only comes from the relative equality of power, between the consumers and the companies. The comparatively short life-span of the small company, and its above-average chance of bankruptcy, are both proof, and the other side of the coin, of its vulnerability to the market. Too many pundits have claimed these to be signs of weakness, and perhaps in some way they are; but they are weaknesses that serve society rather than damage it. The small firm survives only as long as it is providing what the customers want; if it misjudges the market, over-prices its goods, or offers shoddy quality, it fails; and ceases to exist.

If this is weakness, then it is a failing that would have restrained the less prudent excesses of such companies as ITT, Ford, Distillers Co., Shell, BP, and many others. The failings of these corporate giants were allowed to continue simply because they were not vulnerable, they did not have any weakness to the market. They could perform their various misdeeds—ranging from Thalidomide, to knowingly manufacturing dangerous cars, to the overthrow of the elected government of Chile—and then continue business as normal. Their attitude to the ensuring public outcry ranged from silent indifference to banal public relations statements. No small company could have survived the ferocity of public reaction that these corporations generated, and if *only* for that reason, no small firm would have attempted such behaviour.

The weakness of the small firm is the strength of its economy, just as the strength of the big company is the weakness of the monopoly economy. As Engels might have pointed out, through the dialectical process, everything is converted into its opposite: he would probably have ignored the fact that in the preceding sentence, 'strength' and 'weakness' are used in two different senses.

Furthermore, the small firm need not have the traditional capitalist structure of management, ownership, and workers, as three entirely separate groups. First, it is more likely to have a structure where management and owners are the same group, and this group is usually located in the same plant as the workforce. This is instead of the big business situation where management is often physically separated from the workforce, while the shareholders are totally divorced from the whole process, and have no involvement whatsoever. The physical proximity of the small firm makes personal contact and personal relationships much more common, and management is usually conducted on a negotiation basis, rather than dictates and orders. There are exceptions—usually involving firms operating within big business economies—but industrial relations in most small firms are exemplary.

This places the management under an additional constraint; the desire not to upset a congenial workforce for the sake of short-term gains. And the high probability of friendly personal relationships developing creates yet another constraint; the desire to maintain good relationships with workers who are more than just employees. In other words, the simple human wish to keep things on a friendly basis.

The second type of structure is where management, owners, and workers are just one group—as in a co-operative. The workers own the factory—or shop, or whatever—and run it themselves. They do the work, make the managerial decisions, and share the profits. It is the perfect operating example of Marx's proposal that the individuals themselves control the factors of production, *"as the communists desire"*.

In Britain co-operatives have had a somewhat unimpressive history; many of those that have been formed in the last few years have failed, primarily because of government indifference. Due to blocking tactics by politicians or civil servants, co-operatives have been given just enough money for short-term survival—but not enough for investment programmes to cure the faults in the company that led to the creation of the co-op.

But it is important to note that co-operatives are the only practical way to achieve both the spirit and the letter of Marx's goal, that the workers control the means of production themselves. Also, it is only practical in small firms, up to 500 workers. The larger the firm, the more complex are the variety of decisions that have to be made, therefore there is more scope for differences of opinion. The only way to resolve such conflict is by the ballot box, but democratic though this is, it still allows up to 49% of the workforce to be ignored. Owing to the frequent and complex decisions that must be made, it is quite possible that in a large co-op, *none* of the workforce would be entirely satisfied with the way the firm was run. And the larger the co-op, the greater the probability of this being true.

Nonetheless, the small firm, especially the co-operative, represents the only practical solution to the problems that Marx sought to resolve, and the only way of following the major ideals that he stated. Marx's proposals were generally so vague as to allow almost anything to exist; but where he was specific—as with centralisation—the result, when put into practice, could only be authoritarian.

There is no scientific validity for the laws he claimed to have discovered, and the historical progress from declining capitalism, through the transitional phase, to communism, just does not occur in the way that he stated. Nor are his economic theories valid; Marxist-based economies are successful only according to the degree that they eliminate traditional Marxist policies.

And the final paradox, the only practical way to follow the spirit and the letter of Marx's proposals is a structure that is actually a variant of capitalism. It is the final disproof of Marxism.

Clearly it is time to dispose of this aged and outmoded philosophy, and seek newer, more practical answers. Systems that are genuinely egalitarian, and give the worker the freedom and independence that Marx had aimed for; but could never provide.

Recommended Reading

The Theory and Practice of Communism
  R.N. Carew Hunt, Penguin Books.

Karl Marx
  Isiah Berlin, Oxford University Press.

Capitalism and Modern Social Theory
  Anthony Giddens, Cambridge University Press.

Popper
  Bryan Magee, Fontana.

Marxism: An Autopsy
  Henry Bamford Parkes, Chicago University Press.

The Open Society and its Enemies. Vol 2
  Karl Popper, Routledge Kegan Paul.

The Gulag Archipelago
  Alexander Solzhenitsyn, Fontana.

The God that Failed
  Richard Crossman (Ed.), Hamish Hamilton.

Bureaucracy and Revolution in Eastern Europe
  Chris Harman, Pluto Press.

Self-Management on Trial
  Milojko Drulovic, Spokesman.

Gramsci's Marxism
  Carl Boggs, Pluto Press.